Museums of Los Angeles

Westholme Museum Guides

Museums of Atlanta

Museums of Boston

Museums of Chicago

Museums of Los Angeles

Museums of New York City

Museums of Philadelphia

Museums of San Francisco

Museums of Washington, DC

Visiting museums is one of the best ways to get to know a city.
Westholme Museum Guides, designed for both residents and visitors,
are the first-ever uniform compilations of permanent collections open
to the public in America's major cities. Each city has its own unique
group of museums, some famous, others practically unknown, but all
of them are important parts of our nation's cultural life.

Museums of Los Angeles

A Guide for Residents and Visitors

Mia Cariño & Ann Cross

WESTHOLME
Yardley

Acknowledgments

We wish to thank the museum staff members and volunteers who graciously shared valuable information and insights about their institutions. We are grateful to Bruce H. Franklin for the opportunity to write this book and for his patience and encouragement along the way. We also wish to recognize the support of our families and friends, especially those who accompanied us on museum visits and offered helpful editorial advice. And very special thanks to Erik.

Published by Westholme Publishing, LLC, Eight Harvey Avenue, Yardley, Pennsylvania 19067.

Maps by Joseph John Clark

10 9 8 7 6 5 4 3 2 1
First Printing

ISBN 10: 1-59416-027-9

ISBN 13: 978-159416-027-1

www.westholmepublishing.com

Printed in the United States of America on acid-free paper.

For Grant Cariño Shveima

For Gary and Sandy Cross

Contents

Introduction

Los Angeles has come a long way since Gaspar de Portolá (1734–1784) first entered the fertile river valley where the city now stands. Upon his historic landing in 1769, he couldn't have foreseen the urban sprawl that would transform the verdant frontier that lay before him. In turn, it takes effort for any of us to picture how the City of Angels, a culturally vibrant metropolis, was ever an expanse of undeveloped land.

The diarist on Portolá's expedition, a Franciscan priest named Juan Crespi (1721–1782), observed that the Los Angeles basin was a "delightful place." His outlook was, of course, formed in the context of Spain's imperial pursuits, yet his words ring true of the city that has come to be—and of the many museums to be found here. In this book, we have aimed to illuminate some of these great delights, which abound in collections and exhibitions across greater Los Angeles.

Local officials like to report that there are more museums per capita in Los Angeles County than any other in the United States. For this book, we have explored 123 of them and have described what museumgoers can expect to see during their visits. Representing an eclectic mix of subject matter—from European paintings to toy bunnies, fashion to so-called

"Jurassic technology"—the museums of Los Angeles each offer something unique.

Larger institutions such as the Natural History Museum or the Museum of Contemporary Art may come to mind first, but we encourage readers to visit the low-key venues as well. In particular, the modest but well-intentioned museums operated by historical societies reveal Los Angeles one neighborhood at a time. Some of the stories they tell may not seem of consequence, but they add dimension to our understanding of the county as a whole. For us, it's been fun digging into the details—from where the city of Burbank got its name, to how the Santa Anita Race Track came to be, to when Hermosa Beach began its longstanding love affair with beach volleyball.

At 4,000 square miles, Los Angeles County encompasses 88 incorporated cities, chief among them the city that shares its name. The historic heart of this metropolitan region is memorialized at El Pueblo de Los Angeles Historical Monument, in the midst of downtown. It was on this site, in September of 1781, that El Pueblo de Nuestra Señora la Reina de los Ángeles—or Town of Our Lady the Queen of the Angels—was founded in the name of Spain. Today this birthplace is home to three museums—the Avila Adobe, the Plaza Fire House Museum, and the Chinese American Museum—each of which illustrates a different facet of life in the pueblo.

About 11 miles due east, the San Gabriel Mission endures from the Mission Era, a significant chapter in California history. Established in 1771 and eventually supported by the pueblo, it was the fourth of 21 missions founded by Junipero Serra along the Pacific Coast. Aside from the centuries-old church and its cemetery, the grounds now include a museum of devotional art and literature, farming tools, and other objects from everyday life. A visit here—and to the San Fernando Mission, located northwest of the pueblo—is a must for anyone wishing to delve into California's Spanish past.

Representing Native American, European, and African ancestries, the 44 *pobladores* who settled Los Angeles set the stage for the large, multicultural society that would emerge in the city's first 150 years. As rule of the pueblo passed from Spanish to Mexican hands in 1821—followed by California statehood in 1850—the population of Los Angeles steadily increased in the 19th century. For a comprehensive study of the opportunities, both real and mythologized, that lured thousands to California in the 1800s, the Museum of the American West offers important insights. Here and at various history-based museums in town, visitors learn the reasons why people flocked to Los Angeles during this time—to head up ranchos on land grants from the Mexican government following independence from Spain; to start a Quaker colony, as one finds out at the Whittier Museum; to try one's luck down south after striking gold (or striking out) up north; and so on. Delaware native Phineas Banning (1830–1885) arrived almost flat broke in 1851, but he made his mark as the founder of the Port of Los Angeles, one of the most bustling in the world today. His Greek Revival–style mansion—one of several historic house museums to be admired throughout Los Angeles—is preserved as the Banning Residence Museum, just a short distance from the harbor.

Several museums in town celebrate the histories and heritages of the ethnic or cultural groups that have made Los Angeles their home well into the 20th century. The California African American Museum traces the westward migrations of African Americans in the decades after Emancipation and

Reconstruction. The Korean American Museum and the Ararat-Eskijian Museum serve the largest communities of Koreans and Armenians, respectively, outside their homelands. At the Skirball Cultural Center, a distinguished collection of Judaica is a springboard for making connections between the American Jewish experience and that of diverse immigrant groups.

Los Angeles was the adopted hometown of a handful of famed industrialists. Their eminent collections of art have enriched the city. Among these towering figures was railroad baron Henry E. Huntington (1850–1927), who built an extensive interurban transit system for Los Angeles in the early 1900s. Huntington bequeathed his trove of rare books and paintings to the San Marino–based educational institution he established towards the end of his life. Art connoisseur Norton Simon (1907–1993), meanwhile, was the leader of a multinational corporation that included Hunt-Wesson Foods and McCall's Publishing. His eye for Old Master, Impressionist, and Modern works resulted in one of the finest private art collections in the world today. The works of art amassed by oil executives Armand Hammer (1898–1990) and J. Paul Getty (1892–1976) also laid the foundations for the museums that bear their names.

Art enthusiasts should also plan repeat visits to the encyclopedic Los Angeles County Museum of Art, which collects and interprets art from all corners of the globe. To see more of the best of non-Western artistic expression, the Pacific Asia Museum, the Museum of Latin American Art, and the UCLA Fowler Museum of Cultural History should not be missed. With more than 350,000 objects — including basketry, textiles, and pottery — the Southwest Museum of the

American Indian is a major repository for the art and artifacts of America's first peoples. Dating back to 1907, it was the first museum to be founded in Los Angeles. Out in the Mojave Desert, the Antelope Valley Indian Museum houses its own holdings of Native American art in an extraordinary structure built into granite boulders.

While some business giants helped to make Los Angeles a center for great art, George C. Page — the man who popularized the fruit basket — invested in a science museum that would care for Los Angeles's premiere natural treasure: the La Brea Tar Pits. With more than three million Ice Age fossils, the Page Museum takes Angelenos and tourists back to when mammoths ruled the landscape. If prehistoric life is of interest, one should also head east to Claremont, to the Webb Schools' Raymond M. Alf Museum of Paleontology. America's only accredited museum on a high school campus, this institution holds more than 70,000 specimens, nearly all excavated by students and teachers. The California Science Center, one of several museums in Exposition Park, is also a perfect destination for science lovers.

Of course, there is no place like Los Angeles for museums dedicated to the entertainment industry. While no longer the site of the legendary motion-picture studios, the Hollywood district boasts a number of attractions concentrating on American film and television. Among them is the Hollywood Museum, located inside the beautifully restored Max Factor building. Here visitors can walk on the hair-raising set of Hannibal Lecter's cell from *The Silence of the Lambs* and see wardrobe, props, scripts, and more from some of Tinseltown's most famous productions. A few blocks north is the Lasky-DeMille Barn, now home to the Hollywood Heritage

Museum. It was here where Cecil B. DeMille shot the first feature-length film to come out of Hollywood. In Burbank, right on the studio lot, the Warner Bros. Museum exhibits memorabilia illustrating the company's many decades of success.

The presence of Hollywood can be felt in museums beyond those focusing on entertainment. Even in the humble Chatsworth Museum, a display case notes that the rugged terrain of the Chatsworth area made it to the silver screen in *Stagecoach*, starring John Wayne, among other films. The Los Angeles Police Museum, meanwhile, highlights the television classics *Dragnet* and *Adam-12*, both of which featured Los Angeles–based law-enforcement agents working their beats.

Finally, for the youngest museumgoers, Los Angeles offers a wealth of age-appropriate museum experiences. These playfully interactive venues teach everything from plate tectonics to principles of tolerance. In addition to those designed specifically for children, such as the Kidspace Children's Museum, many institutions have committed space and resources to creating kid-friendly galleries or learning centers. In 2007, Los Angeles will enjoy the opening of two long-anticipated destinations for children: the relocated Children's Museum of Los Angeles and the Skirball Cultural Center's new family destination based on the themes of the Noah's Ark story.

We hope that readers will find, as we did, that discovering Los Angeles through the lens of its museums affords a spectacular new view of the city and its environs. For us, it has been a lively and truly rewarding way to come to love, even more, the place that we call home.

Using *Museums of Los Angeles*

For the purposes of this book, a museum is defined as a permanent collection, open to the public, of predominantly nonreproduction artifacts. Exceptions have been made for a few historic houses with limited or no permanent collection because of their architectural significance and/or their survival from Los Angeles's earliest days. Exceptions have also been made for a few museums that do not maintain permanent collections, such as the Santa Monica Museum of Art and the Zimmer Children's Museum, since they function primarily as exhibiting institutions and offer visitors a gallery-based experience.

The museums are listed in alphabetical order by the primary name of the museum or collection. Each entry provides the address, phone number, and Web site for the museum, as well as the hours of operation, admission prices and policies, and parking instructions. This information is always subject to change, especially at the smaller museums where day-to-day operations depend heavily on the availability of volunteers. Calling ahead or checking the Web site is strongly advised. Doing so will also inform you of temporary exhibitions and special programs, which may require special ticketing.

Many museums do not charge an admission fee, but donations are almost always welcome and appreciated even when one is not suggested. Many museums offer free admission on particular days or times of the week; to find out about these special hours, please see the museum entries. We encourage readers who intend to visit museums more often—or who simply want to support an institution in its mission—to consider museum membership. Membership typically offers a wealth of benefits, including free year-round admission, sneak previews of exhibitions, and discounts at gift shops.

Included in the book are several maps. Each museum is represented on the maps by the page number of its corresponding entry. This enables readers to see which museums are located near each other and therefore which ones could reasonably be visited in one trip.

Each entry also features quick-reference symbols meant to highlight important points about a museum, such as whether it has been designed specifically for young audiences or whether food is available on the premises. A key to all of these symbols is at the end of this section.

In a book about Los Angeles, a town so reliant on the automobile, it was imperative to include a symbol indicating whether a museum is reachable by public transportation. Of course, every museum is reachable by car—with the sole exception of Catalina Island Museum, to which one must ride a ferry. Exact driving directions from major thoroughfares are often provided on each museum's Web site. The various online map resources also come in handy. If we have indicated that public transportation is an option for a particular museum, it means that the museum is within a 1/3-mile walk from a bus or train stop serviced by the Metropolitan Transit Authority. Some destinations may be harder to reach than others, but we encourage readers to get out from behind the wheel, make use of these mass-transit options, and delight in the sites you may see along the way.

Following the museum entries is a section that organizes the museums into different categories, such as the essential museums for children and the top venues for art or science.

Finally, we hope that readers will take the time to visit the myriad other destinations throughout Los Angeles that would not be included in a book of this type, including the Los

Angeles Zoo, the Aquarium of the Pacific, the Los Angeles County Arboretum and Botanic Garden, and the Griffith Park Observatory. Also excluded from the book are the iconic Watts Towers, a landmark work of folk art by Simon Rodia, and the many examples of public art that animate the cityscape. All of these are important Los Angeles attractions well worth the time to visit.

Further Reading and Resources

Davis, Mike. *City of Quartz: Excavating the Future in Los Angeles*. Vintage Books USA, 1992.

O'Connor, Letitia Burns. *Discover Los Angeles: An Informed Guide to L.A.'s Rich and Varied Cultural Life*. Getty Publications, 1998.

Pitt, Leonard and Dale Pitt. *Los Angeles A to Z: An Encyclopedia to the City and County*. University of California Press, 1997.

Poole, Jean Bruce and Tevvy Ball. *El Pueblo: The Historic Heart of Los Angeles*. Getty Publications, 2002.

Visitor Information

Los Angeles Visitor Information Center
685 Figueroa Street, Los Angeles
213-689-8822
www.seemyla.com
Open: Daily, 9:00 AM–5:00 PM

Located in the heart of downtown, this walk-up visitor information center is operated by LA Inc., the city's convention and visitors bureau. It's where to pick up an official visitor's kit and find out what to do, where to stay, and how to get around. For those wishing to cover a lot of ground in just a few days, LA

Inc.'s "See My LA GO Los Angeles Card" may be a good deal. Available for purchase in 1, 2, 3, 5, or 7-day increments, the all-access pass provides free general admission to more than 30 attractions—including many of the museums profiled in this book—as well as discounts at shops and restaurants. LA Inc.'s Web site is also packed with useful information.

Hollywood Visitor Information Center

6801 Hollywood Boulevard, Los Angeles
323-467-6412
www.seemyla.com
Open: M–Sa, 10:00 AM–10:00 PM; Su, 10:00 AM–7:00 PM

Like the one on Figueroa Street, this walk-up visitor information center—just steps away from the Kodak Theater, home of the Oscars—is operated by LA Inc. It offers the same services and special promotions. See above for details.

Pasadena Visitors Center

171 S. Robles Avenue, Pasadena
626-795-9311 or toll-free 1-800-307-7977
www.pasadenacal.com
Open: M–F, 8:00 AM–5:00 PM; Sa, 10:00 AM–4:00 PM

Santa Monica Visitor Information Center

1920 Main Street, Suite B, Santa Monica
310-393-7593 or toll-free at 1-800-544-5319
www.santamonica.com
Open: Daily, 9:00 AM–6:00 PM

ExperienceLA

www.experiencela.com

This free online resource provides information about cultural destinations throughout greater Los Angeles and features a calendar of events. Users can also view maps, look up suggested itineraries, take advantage of special promotions, and obtain information about public transit.

Regional Transportation

Despite its reputation as a city best traveled by car, Los Angeles County has one of the largest public transportation systems in the country, the "Metro." The Metro's network of buses and trains serves the entire region, and the easy-to-use Metro Trip Planner on its Web site is particularly helpful to make your way around the city.

METRO (Los Angeles County Metropolitan Transportation Authority)
One Gateway Plaza, Los Angeles
1-800-COMMUTE (1-800-266-6883)
www.mta.net

Downloadable maps and timetables are available at Metro's Web site, which provides the most current information about bus and rail schedules.

Maps

Each museum in this book is marked on the following maps by its page number. These maps are designed to show the reader the general proximity of the museums to one another.

Museums of Los Angeles

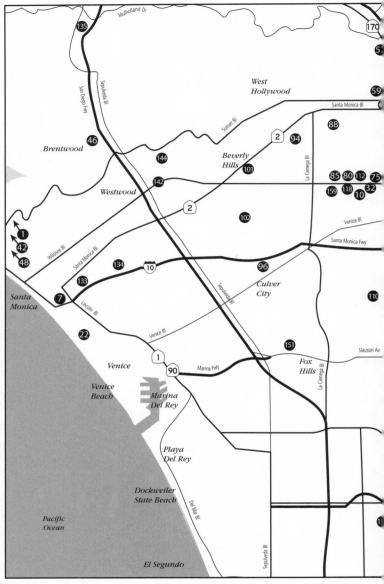

Map No. 1: Museums on the West Side and Central Los Angeles.

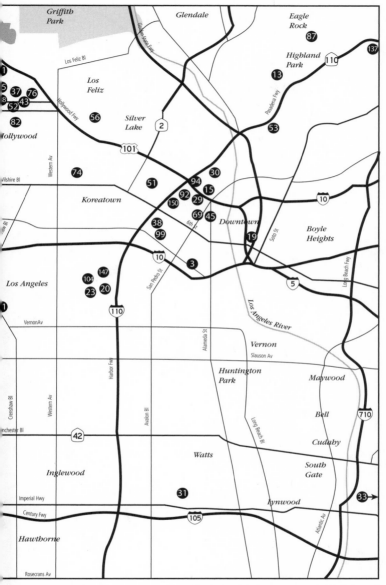

(Each number is a museum's book page.)

Map No. 2: Museums in the San Fernando Valley

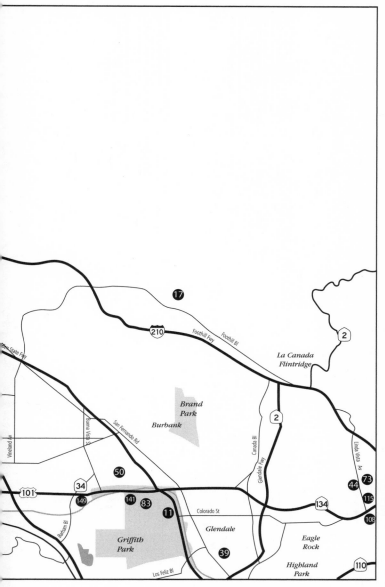

(Each number is a museum's book page.)

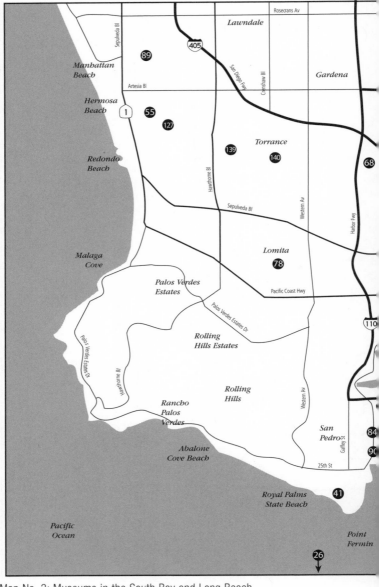

Map No. 3: Museums in the South Bay and Long Beach

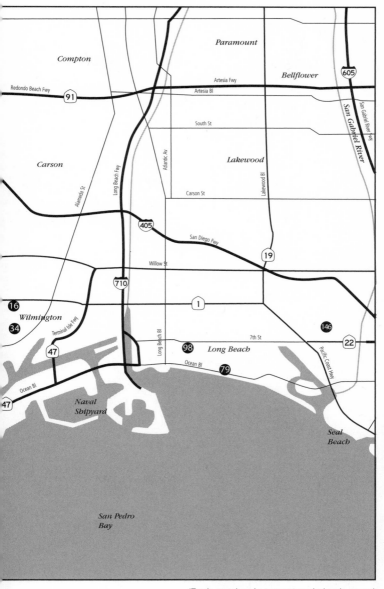

(Each number is a museum's book page.)

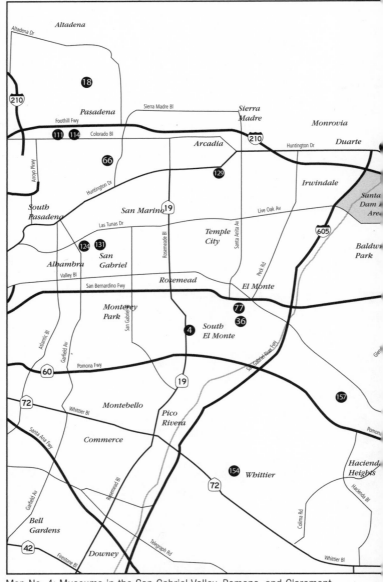

Map No. 4: Museums in the San Gabriel Valley, Pomona, and Claremont

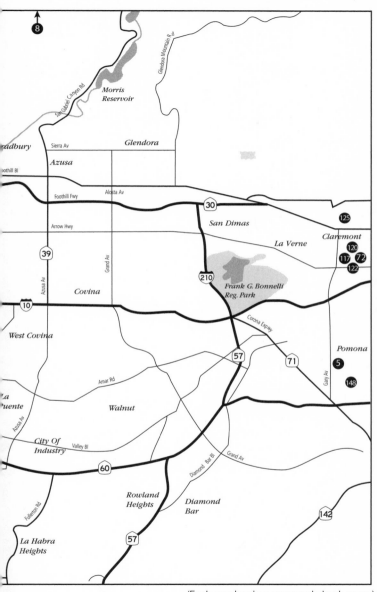

(Each number is a museum's book page.)

Visual Codes

Architecturally significant

Exhibits suitable for children

Reachable by public transportation

Food available on premises

Must call ahead

Notable art

Notable grounds or garden

Science oriented

Site of historic event

Adamson House and Malibu Lagoon Museum

23200 Pacific Coast Highway, Malibu (Map No. 1)
310-456-8432
www.adamsonhouse.org

Open: House (note: access to house by guided tour only) and museum—W–Sa, 11:00 AM–3:00 PM; grounds only—daily from sunrise to sunset; garden tour at 10:00 AM on Friday
Admission: Free to museum and grounds; for access and guided tour of house—Adults, $5.00; Children 6–16, $2.00; Children under 6, Free; for garden tour—General, $5.00
Parking: Pay parking in nearby lots

The early California people known as the Chumash once inhabited a seaside village they called Humaliwo, meaning "the surf sounds lovely," where this historic house and museum now stand. With waves crashing in the near distance, visitors here today will delight in the picturesque residence of Mr. and Mrs. Merritt Adamson, founders of the Adohr dairy farms. Designed in the Spanish Colonial Revival style by architect Stiles O. Clements, the 1930s residence boasts thousands of brilliant tiles produced by the Malibu Potteries company, which was owned and operated for its six productive years (1926–1932) by Mrs. Adamson's mother, May Knight Rindge. The abundance of tile—adorning the interior spaces as well as the pool, garden paths, courtyard, and fountains—complements the house's decoratively painted walls and ceilings and fancy ironwork. The rooms contain the Adamsons' original furniture as well as their kitchenware, china, linens, and books. Some of their clothes are even hanging in the closets. The museum, set up in the adjacent five-car garage building, exhibits a collection of Chumash artifacts, as well as photographs and documents shedding light on the history of Malibu, the lives of the Rindges and Adamsons, and the great success of Malibu Potteries.

Highlight:

A Persian-style "rug" painted into the tile, complete with fringed edges

The African American Firefighter Museum

1401 S. Central Avenue, Los Angeles (Map No. 1)
213-744-1730
www.aaffmuseum.org

Open: Tu and Th, 10:00 AM–2:00 PM; Su, 1:00–4:00 PM
Admission: Free
Parking: Free in museum lot; also street parking

Dating back more than 100 years, the service of African Americans in the Los Angeles Fire Department (LAFD) is commemorated at this museum, which dwells inside the restored Los Angeles Fire Station #30. The station, founded in 1913, first served as an all-white facility but later became, between the years of 1924 and 1955, one of two segregated fire stations in Los Angeles fully operated by African Americans. Visitors to the museum will find a 1940 Pirsch ladder truck, as well as badges, helmets, photographs, and other artifacts and memorabilia. The important role of African American women in the LAFD is illustrated in a special display. Also given emphasis are the experiences of the Old Stentorians, firemen who worked during the challenging periods of segregation and desegregation.

American Military Vehicle Museum

1918 N. Rosemead Boulevard, Whittier Narrows Recreation Area,
South El Monte (Map No. 4)
626-442-1776
www.hometown.aol.com/tankland/museum.htm

Open: F–Su, 10:00 AM–4:30 PM; closed on rainy days
Admission: Adults, $4.00; Veterans and Seniors, $3.00; Children
10–16, $2.00; Children 5–9, $0.50; Children under 5, Free
Parking: Free in museum lot

Spend the day outdoors at this repository for retired and
restored U.S. military vehicles and artillery. More than 170
holdings, almost all dating from World War II or later, line the
dirt paths of the museum's grounds — tanks, trucks, helicopters,
jeeps, ambulances, anti-aircraft artillery, and other military
transportation and equipment. Among the more extraordinary
items are one of the 2,000-pound bombs dropped during
Desert Storm; armed recovery vehicles built to reclaim disabled
tanks and trucks in battle; and a landing craft used to retrieve
personnel or equipment during amphibious operations in
Vietnam. A handy booklet informs visitors of the history of
each vehicle on the premises, including its key statistics, such as
weight, speed, and power. Moviegoers may notice the Soviet
surface-to-air missile battery mock-up used in the movie *The
Sum of All Fears*, while fans of *M*A*S*H* will recognize the
military ambulance featured in both the original film and the
long-running television series.

American Museum of Ceramic Art

340 S. Garey Avenue, Pomona (Map No. 4)
909-865-3146
www.ceramicmuseum.org

Open: W–Sa, Noon–5:00 PM; second Saturday of every month,
Noon–10:00 PM
Admission: Free
Parking: Street parking

Founded to promote the appreciation of clay as an art form,
this young museum opened its doors in the fall of 2004 and
since then has mounted a number of temporary shows. These
have exhibited the work of both renowned and emerging clay
artists while tracking significant achievements in ceramic technology worldwide, from ancient times to the present.
Exhibition labels bring attention to the construction, glazing,
and firing practices used in creating the works, as well as their
shapes, forms, and styles of decoration. Every exhibition features a companion video, screened on continuous loop right in
the galleries, and, when possible, includes items from the museum's permanent collection, which is sure to grow in coming
years as the museum's acquisitions policy is developed and
refined. Contemporary studio pottery will certainly remain a
staple of the collection.

Highlights:

Approximately 50 works by printmaker and ceramics master
Paul Soldner

A group of functional as well as sculptural works by Don Reitz

Andres Pico Adobe

10940 Sepulveda Boulevard, Mission Hills (Map No. 2)
818-365-7810
www.sfvhs.com

Open: M, 10:00 AM–3:00 PM; third Sunday of every month,
1:00–4:00 p.m.
Admission: Free
Parking: Free in museum lot

A few miles from the San Fernando Mission, this historic
building is the second oldest adobe home still standing in Los
Angeles (the oldest is the Avila Adobe; see p. 15). The oldest
portion of the structure was erected around 1834, after Mexico
gained independence from Spain and secured control of the ex-
Mission lands. In 1846, ownership of the house, along with the
entire San Fernando Valley, transferred to Spaniard Eulogio de
Celis when Mexico failed to repay funds borrowed from him to
finance its war against the United States. It was likely de Celis
who added the dining room and library to the one-room adobe.
In 1853, Mexican cattle rancher and army general Andres Pico
took over 2,000 acres of de Celis's land, including the house.
Pico never lived here, but in 1874, his adopted children moved
into the adobe and expanded it to include a kitchen, two wings,
and the second floor. After they moved out, in the late 1800s, it
gradually fell into disrepair—until archaeologist Mark
Harrington restored it in the 1930s. Today the adobe is furnished in late-Victorian style. Only two 1870s Majolica dishes
remain of the original furnishings but throughout the house are
photographs, costumes, household items, and other objects to
give a sense of the bygone Mission and Spanish-Mexican eras.

Angels Attic

516 Colorado Avenue, Santa Monica (Map No. 1)

310-394-8331

www.angelsattic.com

Open: Th–Su, 12:30–4:30 PM

Admission: Adults, $6.50; Seniors, $4.00; Children under 12, $3.50

Parking: Street parking

A stately, two-story Queen Anne house built in 1895 is the fitting home of this museum of antique dollhouses, miniatures, and dolls. The rooms are filled with more than 60 meticulously furnished and generously accessorized dollhouses from around the world, spanning a range of architectural styles. Many date back to before World War II. Visitors will find inlaid floors, stained glass, chandeliers, rococo ceilings, wallpaper, porcelain decorative arts, and other fine details in many of the miniature homes and shops. While visiting, enjoy afternoon tea and assorted homemade sweets on the enclosed verandah or in the garden's gazebo. If you come by around Christmas, you'll find the exterior of Angels Attic and every dollhouse on display seasonally decorated. Museum proceeds benefit children living with autism and other developmental disabilities.

Highlights:

A three-room dollhouse owned by Johanna Spyri, author of *Heidi*

A seven-foot-tall Mexican mansion, built circa 1890 in the style of large homes constructed at that time in Mexico City and Puebla

Antelope Valley Indian Museum

Avenue M between East 150th and 170th Streets, Lancaster
(Map No. 4)
661-942-0662
www.avim.parks.ca.gov

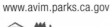

Open: Mid-September through mid-June, Sa–Su, 11:00 AM–4:00 PM;
closed during the summer
Admission: Adults 18 and up, $2.00; Children under 18, Free
Parking: Free in museum lot

As if growing out of the rugged terrain, the one-of-a-kind
structure that houses this museum integrates the large granite
boulders on which it stands, both inside and out. The chalet-
style building was the home of Hollywood set decorator and
artist H. Arden Edwards, who had long desired to live in the
Mojave Desert's scenic Antelope Valley embraced by mighty
rock formations. And so beginning in 1928, he built the five-
room residence, reserving the upper floor as a place to display
his treasures of Native American art. Today it is a museum
dedicated to educating the public about prehistoric, historic,
and contemporary Indian cultures of the western Great Basin,
California, Arizona, and New Mexico. Expanding upon
Edwards's collection, the museum's holdings of rugs, baskets,
pottery, jewelry, clothing, and stone tools provide insight into
how various early peoples lived in the Antelope Valley.
Emphasis is placed on the major role the region played as a
trade route connecting the coast, the desert, and the mountains. Visitors may also wish to hike the museum's half-mile
nature trail to admire the desert landscape that so enchanted
Edwards.

Ararat-Eskijian Museum

15105 Mission Hills Road, Mission Hills (Map No. 2)
818-838-4862
www.ararat-eskijian-museum.com
Open: Sa–Su, 1:00–5:00 PM; first Tuesday of every month, 1:00–3:00 PM
Admission: Free; donations encouraged
Parking: Free in facility lot; also street parking

Armenian heritage is preserved at this museum, founded in 1993 by Luther Eskijian. As the only Armenian museum on the West Coast, it aims to serve the more than 300,000 Armenians who live in greater Los Angeles, the largest Armenian community outside the homeland. Eskijian's collection of ancient artifacts, documents, coins, art, and books forms the basis of the museum's holdings. These are continually augmented by new acquisitions and gifts from Armenian families wanting to safeguard their heirlooms for future generations. The works of art are many and varied, ranging from the period of the Hittites (1800–800 BCE) to handwoven textiles from the 1800s to an oil painting by the late 20th-century Pasadena artist Jirayr Zorthian. Also in the collection are illuminated manuscripts, musical instruments, stamps, national costumes, rugs, and maps revealing the shifting borders of Armenia throughout history. Many documents and objects, complementing the resources in the adjacent library, relate to the Armenian Genocide of 1915, most strikingly a case of human bone fragments found in the Syrian desert.

Highlights:

The courtyard bronze statue, *Mother Armenia Rising Out of the Ashes,* by Harout Halebian

Bust of Armenian American George Deukmejian (1983–1991), the 35th Governor of California

Architecture + Design Museum

5900 Wilshire Boulevard, Suite 100E, Los Angeles (Map No. 1)
323-932-9393
www.aplusd.org
Open: M–Sa, 10:00 AM–6:00 PM; Su, 11:00 AM–5:00 PM
Admission: Free
Parking: Pay parking in facility garage; also, pay parking in nearby lots
and street parking

Nicknamed the "A plus D," this museum probes contemporary issues in architecture, urbanism, and design and seeks to encourage innovation in these disciplines. Its changing exhibitions showcase the work of important architects of regional, national, and international acclaim as well as major figures in interior, landscape, product, and fashion design. Past shows have highlighted works by Richard Neutra, Edward Tufte, and Ray Kappe. After several fruitful seasons at a location downtown and then in West Hollywood, the museum has just relocated to "Museum Row," on Wilshire Boulevard, opposite the Los Angeles County Museum of Art. The A+D will continue its programming and may also start building a permanent collection of drawings, models, and photographs.

Autry National Center: Museum of the American West

4700 Western Heritage Way, Griffith Park, Los Angeles (Map No. 2)
323-667-2000
www.autrynationalcenter.org

Open: Tu–W and F–Su, 10:00 AM–5:00 PM; Th, 10:00 AM–8:00 PM
Admission: Adults, $7.50; Seniors and Students, $5.00; Children
2–12, $3.00; also, free general admission on Thursdays, 4:00–8:00
PM, and all day on second Tuesday of every month
Parking: Free in museum lot

Drive into Griffith Park and venture into the American
West—its interwoven histories, cultures, diverse peoples, and
complex mythologies. This museum, founded by entertainment
legend Gene Autry, tells of the region west of the Mississippi
River, from its prehistoric roots to the present. Its collection of
more than 78,000 works of art and artifacts illuminates the lives
of the Spanish explorers, brings to life the Gold Rush and
other westward paths of opportunity, and chronicles formative
moments in the post–Civil War period, such as the completion
of the transcontinental railroad. One gallery depicts ranch life,
presenting spurs, branding irons, saddles, and dress used by
cowboys throughout the ages, from early Spanish *vaqueros* to
modern ranchers. Attention is given throughout to the many
immigrant groups that settled in the West. Alongside this
authentic history, the museum sheds light on the fictional
American West, as created and popularized in such extravagan-
zas as Buffalo Bill's Wild West Shows, as well as in radio, film,
and television. Props, movie posters, costumes, original screenplays, merchandise, and even a stage set of a Western street

scene reveal the impact of Hollywood on popular perceptions of the West. Also on view are Western-genre paintings, sculpture by Charles M. Russell and Frederic Remington, and decorative arts from the 19th and 20th centuries.

Additional highlights:

The Colt Firearms Collection

A handdrawn diagram by Wyatt Earp of the shoot-out at the OK Corral

Gene Autry "Singing Cowboy" memorabilia

Autry National Center: Southwest Museum of the American Indian

234 Museum Drive, Los Angeles (Map No. 1)

323-221-2164

www.autrynationalcenter.org

Open: Sa–Su, Noon–5:00 PM

Admission: Free

Parking: Free in museum lot

Established in 1907 and recently made part of the Autry National Center, this anthropological institution in Mt. Washington is the oldest museum in the city of Los Angeles. Inspirited by founder Charles F. Lummis — the photographer, journalist, historian, and fervent devotee to Southwestern culture and tradition — the museum studies American Indian history, especially of the West, through its significant collection of art and artifacts spanning more than two millennia. The material culture held by the museum hails from the many American Indian societies that have lived within California's borders, along the northwest coast — from Northern California to Alaska — and on the Great Plains. Past exhibits have looked at how native art traditions have continually evolved in the Southwest with the influx of new influences, including that of the Navajo and Apache who migrated from Canada and drew inspiration from Pueblo design.

In mid-2006, the museum closed its doors in order to rehabilitate its landmark white adobe building and to focus on properly conserving its 350,000 objects, encompassing basketry, pottery, textiles, beadwork, costumes, tools, and paintings. During the renovation, the museum will greet visitors only during the weekends for educational events while much of its collection will be relocated to the Autry National Center's Museum of the American West. To learn more about the changes to both facilities of the Autry National Center, check the Web site.

Avila Adobe

10 Olvera Street, Los Angeles (Map No. 1)
213-628-1274
www.cityofla.org/ELP/avila.htm

Open: Daily, 9:00 AM–3:00 PM
Admission: Free
Parking: Pay parking in nearby lots; also street parking

Built in 1818 by Don Francisco Avila, a prosperous cattle rancher and onetime *alcalde* (mayor) of Los Angeles, the Avila Adobe is the oldest existing residence in the city. After Avila's death, in 1832, the building remained, for the most part, in the hands of his family through the 1860s. However, U.S. Commodore Robert F. Stockton made it his headquarters during peace negotiations for the Mexican-American War. It was later converted into a boarding house. In 1926, Christine Sterling, a champion of historic preservation, rescued the house and its surrounding area from condemnation, establishing it as a tourist attraction celebrating the city's Mexican culture and heritage. Today the one-level ranch adobe structure is a museum designed to reflect the Hispanic lifestyle of 1840s California, furnished as it might have been during the days of the Avilas, from the master bedroom and the parlor to the kitchen and the office. The Avila Adobe is part of El Pueblo de Los Angeles Historical Monument, which marks the city's birthplace.

Highlight:

The original black lacquer lacemaker of Avila's second wife, Doña Encarnación

Banning Residence Museum

401 East "M" Street, Wilmington (Map No. 3)
310-548-7777
www.banningmuseum.org

Open: Access to house by guided tour only, offered hourly, Tu–Th,
12:30–2:30 PM, and Sa–Su, 12:30–3:30 PM
Recommended donation: $5.00
Parking: Street parking; also free parking in adjacent lot

In 1851, Phineas Banning (1830–1885) arrived in Southern
California from Wilmington, Delaware, virtually penniless.
Today he is credited with advancing the area's growth and prosperity in the latter part of the 19th century. Known as the father
of the Port of Los Angeles, Banning was instrumental in the
development of the harbor at San Pedro on seemingly ill-suited
land. He also established a railway system from the San Pedro
Bay to Los Angeles and constructed the first telegraph lines to
provide communications between the young city and the rest of
the nation. Fittingly, this stately museum honoring Banning's
visionary, entrepreneurial spirit sits on 20 acres of park in the
area he helped to create. Designed and built by Banning himself
in 1864 — in the Greek Revival style of architecture popular then
in his native Delaware — the 23-room mansion (with 18 rooms
open to the public) is filled with Victorian furnishings, books,
and household objects, including items originally owned by the
Bannings during their residence there. Visitors should take note
of the view from Banning's office, from which he could keep
close watch on the workings of the harbor in the distance. Also
stop by the barn adjacent to the house to see an impressive collection of stagecoaches and carriages from the 19th century, as
well as a fully-stocked smithy.

Bolton Hall Museum

10110 Commerce Avenue, Tujunga (Map No. 2)
818-352-3420
www.verdugo-online.com/clubs/boltonhall.htm

Open: Tu and Su, 1:00–4:00 PM
Admission: Free
Parking: Street parking

In the very early 20th century, an idealist named William E.
Smythe organized "The Little Landers" in the Sunland-
Tujunga area of Los Angeles. The movement's core belief was
that families could subsist on a small parcel of land each and
prosper as a community. In 1913, the Little Landers began set-
tling onto acre and half-acre lots located between the Verdugo
Hills and the San Gabriel Mountains and lived their dream of
cooperative living for several years. Their all-purpose club-
house, Bolton Hall, which was built using river rocks from the
local hillsides and the nearby Tujunga Wash, was where they
held everything from church services to holiday socials.
Although by 1920 the first World War, years of economic
recession, and a growing cynicism among the colonists had
brought an end to the movement, Bolton Hall continued to
serve the area in various capacities for decades. In 1959, when it
faced demolition, local citizens banded together as the Little
Landers Historical Society and successfully battled for its
restoration. Since 1980, the historic stone structure has served
as a museum of photographs, artifacts, documents, and memorabilia of Sunland-Tujunga dating back to its Native American
roots. As far as the building's name goes, Bolton Hall was a
friend of Smythe's, whose writings about land development
inspired the Little Lander philosophy.

The Bunny Museum

1933 Jefferson Drive, Pasadena (Map No. 1)
626-798-8848
www.thebunnymuseum.com

Open: Daily by appointment; no appointment necessary on major holidays but call ahead for specific hours
Admission: Free
Parking: Street parking

On Valentine's Day 1992, Steve Lubanksi gave his "Honey Bunny," Candace Frazee, a snuggly bunny toy. The following Easter, Candace gave Steve a porcelain bunny. The gift exchange soon became a daily event and to this day the Pasadena couple gives one another a bunny item every single day. With a collection multiplying at world-record pace, the couple opened up this museum in their own home in 1998, welcoming visitors into a warren of rabbit-themed collectibles, now totaling more than 20,000. Bunny items of all shapes and sizes and in a variety of media fill the space wall to wall, floor to ceiling—light fixtures, paintings, figurines, marionettes, chimes, you name it. While many are presented in formal display, there are many more used in Candace and Steve's everyday life, such as the telephone, flatware, cutting board—even the toilet plunger. You'll recognize in the collection well-known characters like Thumper, Bugs Bunny, and *Alice in Wonderland*'s White Rabbit. You may also catch a glimpse of several live rabbit pets hopping around freely.

The Cake Lady's® Mini Cake Museum

573 S. Boyle Avenue, Los Angeles (Map No. 1)
323-263-6195
www.hollenbeckhome.com/minicakemuseum.html

Open: By appointment only
Admission: Free
Parking: Free in facility lot

This museum is the icing on the cake of Frances Kuyper's storied career. Since 1950, Kuyper—known lovingly as "The Cake Lady"® by those who've had the pleasure of meeting her—has dedicated herself to the art of cake decorating, serving as a master designer, teacher, and author. Long envisioning a place to share her love of the craft and display the many skillfully ornamented cakes she discovered during her travels, Kuyper first opened her museum in 1994 in her Pasadena home. In 1999, the museum moved with Kuyper to the Hollenbeck Home, a retirement community where she now lives. More than 150 cakes from nine countries showcase a variety of cake-decorating techniques. Wedding, birthday, children's, and other special-occasion cakes—all built upon Styrofoam bases—boast intricate designs and innovative, sculptural use of edible items. On view is a replica of one of Kuyper's first theme cakes, featuring a scarecrow with a graham-cracker body and a marshmallow head surrounded by pretzel cornstalks. There are also cakes decorated, with lifelike realism, in the shapes of animals and people. Cake-decorating demonstrations by Kuyper are occasionally held at the museum; call for information.

California African American Museum

600 State Drive, Los Angeles (Map No. 1)
213-744-7432
www.caamuseum.org

Open: W–Sa, 10:00 AM–4:00 PM; first Sunday of every month, 11:00 AM–5:00 PM
Admission: Free
Parking: Pay parking in Exposition Park lots

More than half of the 44 settlers who founded the pueblo that would become Los Angeles were of African descent, and this museum celebrates the full range of contributions African Americans have made to the development of the United States, in particular the West. Its collections include West African ceremonial objects from the 16th through the 19th centuries. These represent the art and culture of Africans prior to being shipped by the millions to the American South. African American legacy is honored not only through documents of slavery, but through objects revealing the artistry of slaves adept at carpentry, pottery, metalwork, and more. After Emancipation and Reconstruction, conditions for African Americans living in the South became treacherous, so a significant portion of the population moved north and west in search of new opportunities. Museum galleries trace these significant migrations, showing how the African American population in California grew from 8,000 to 40,000 between 1910 and 1930. The contributions of 20th-century African American luminaries—from Ella Fitzgerald to Huey Long to golfer Bill Spiller—are brought to life through key photographs and memorabilia. Also among the museum's holdings are works of art by African American artists, including landscape painter Robert Scott Duncanson and sculptor Artis Lane, as well as contemporary art from the African diaspora.

Highlights:

The official portrait of Tom Bradley, Los Angeles's first and only African American mayor

John Outterbridge's assemblage *Twenty-Two Rhymes in a Row*

A display of West African wood masks, sculpture, and head-dresses

California Heritage Museum

2612 Main Street, Santa Monica (Map No. 1)
310-392-8537
www.californiaheritagemuseum.org

Open: W–Su, 11:00 AM–4:00 PM
Admission: Adults, $5.00; Seniors and Students, $3.00; Children under 12, Free
Parking: Limited free parking in museum lot; also pay parking in nearby lots and street parking

Inside the restored 1894 historic house of Santa Monica civic leader Roy Jones, designated a city landmark in 1979, is this museum of American decorative and folk arts. Its collection of Monterey furniture, Indian pottery and baskets, tile, and kitchenware are exhibited in period room settings designed to showcase the fine craftsmanship of classic California manufacturers such as Mason Manufacturing and Malibu Potteries. Sunday is a great day to visit the museum, when it hosts a popular farmers' market on its landscaped grounds and in the parking lot.

Highlights:

A 1930s-style kitchen, modeled after the one in which would-be entrepreneur and onetime Santa Monica resident Merle Norman launched her cosmetics business

A table fully set with the signature colorful dinnerware by California Rainbow Mayer Company

California Science Center

700 State Drive, Los Angeles (Map No. 1)

323-SCIENCE (323-724-3623)

www.californiasciencecenter.org

Open: Main center—Daily, 10:00 AM–5:00 PM; Sketch Foundation
Gallery—M–F, 10:00 AM–1:00 PM and Sa–Su, 11:00 AM–4:00 PM;
check Web site for IMAX movie schedule

Admission: Free to the permanent exhibits; separate fees for select
attractions and for IMAX theater tickets

Parking: Pay parking in Exposition Park lots

Science lessons are given a spin at this family destination, located in Exposition Park. Blending the façade of its original 1913 building (it was known then as the California Museum of Science and Industry) with a new, modern facility, the 265,000-square-foot center houses hundreds of interactive, playful exhibits linking scientific principles with everyday life. Uniting the first group of galleries is the theme *World of Life*, investigating the basic life processes common to all living things, from single-celled organisms to the 100-trillion-celled human being. Visitors young and old can check out the brains of different species, learn how people, plants, and animals break down food to create energy, view bacteria through microscopes, watch live chicks hatch from eggs, and see how much blood fills the arteries and veins of an elephant. The second permanent exhibit, *Creative World*, celebrates how basic science is at the heart of modern living. Probed here are the inventions and innovations humans have come up with to advance communications, transportation, and structural engineering. In between these main exhibits are even more science-based play stations and galleries for changing exhibitions, including one reserved for exploring the intersection between art and science.

Be sure to venture outside the center's main building to experience the Sketch Foundation Gallery Air and Space Exhibits in an adjacent building and surrounding grounds. Aerospace artifacts and related hands-on activities illustrate principles of air, space, and flight, and the ways these impact aircraft and spacecraft design. Finally, consider seeing the big picture in the center's IMAX theater, the first nonprofit educational 3D theater on the West Coast.

Highlights:

"Tess," a 50-foot animatron that illustrates how muscles, bones, organs, and blood vessels achieve homeostasis

The *Mercury-Redstone 2* and *Gemini 11* space capsules

A high-wire bicycle visitors can pedal three stories above the lobby

Canoga–Owensmouth Historical Museum

7248 Owensmouth Avenue, Canoga Park (Map No. 2)
818-340-3696

Open: Call ahead for hours
Admission: Free
Parking: Free in museum lot

Present-day Canoga Park used to be Owensmouth, so named because of its location near the outlet of the Owens River Aqueduct. Owensmouth was founded in March of 1912 and was given its new name, Canoga Park, in 1930. This museum — which forms part of the Canoga Park Community Center inside the converted 1930s Los Angeles Fire Station #72 — traces the history of the area through documents, photographs, ceramics, costumes, furniture, and jewelry. These memorabilia help piece together the story of Owensmouth/Canoga Park from its beginnings as an agricultural community to its growth into a busy town, which over time established its own schools, library, civic and business organizations, theater, churches, and transportation systems. Much of the material on display tells of the construction and use of the old railroad stop of Owensmouth.

Catalina Island Museum

1 Casino Way, Avalon (Map No. 3)
310-510-2414
www.catalinamuseum.org

Open: April–December, daily, 10:00 AM–4:00 PM; January–March,
F–W, 10:00 AM–4:00 PM
Admission: Adults, $4.00; Seniors, $3.00; Children, $1.00; Children
under 5, Free

Twenty-two miles off the coast of Los Angeles sits picturesque
Santa Catalina Island. Its heritage and history are preserved at
this museum through a collection of approximately 150,000
objects, including archaeological artifacts, historical photographs, newspaper clippings, postcards, and works of art. From
the earliest settlements of Native Americans more than 7,000
years ago to its emergence as a resort destination at the turn of
the 20th century, the museum illustrates Catalina Island's many
changes in ownership, inhabitants, prosperity level, and purpose
of use. Exhibits tell of the steamships that serviced the island
for 100 years as well as its role as a Hollywood "backlot" for
hundreds of movies. There is also a colorful collection of
Catalina pottery and tile, manufactured from rich clay deposits
discovered on the island in the early 1920s. The museum is on
the ground floor of Catalina Island's famous Casino building.
No gambling takes place here; the building takes its name from
the Italian word *casino*, meaning "gathering place."

Highlight:

Material culture of the Native Americans who were evicted
from the island and sent to the San Gabriel Mission on the
mainland in the early 1800s

Chatsworth Museum

10385 Shadow Oak Drive, Chatsworth (Map No. 2)
818-882-5614
www.historicalsocieties.net

Open: First Sunday of every month, 1:00–4:00 PM
Admission: Free
Parking: Free in museum lot

The Tataviam and the Chumash peoples were the first inhabitants of the San Fernando Valley, including the community of Chatsworth. Chatworth's proximity to the steep mountain route known as the Santa Susana Pass made it a high-traffic thoroughfare for 18th- and early 19th-century travelers en route to and from the San Fernando Mission. After Mission life ended, Chatsworth became an active relay station for stagecoaches commuting between Los Angeles and San Francisco during the Gold Rush. The museum keeps a collection of objects and photographs chronicling this history of the Chatsworth area. Docents in 18th-century costume show visitors Native American artifacts found at nearby archaeological digs, as well as personal belongings and snapshots of the early European pioneer families who petitioned for land here as per the Homestead Act of 1862 (the museum itself sits on former property of homesteaders James David and Rhoda Jane Hill). There is also a display of photographs showing the completion of the railroad to Chatsworth and the building of the railroad tunnels through the Santa Susana Mountains (1898–1904). Movie buffs will note that Chatsworth's rocky landscape would later provide an evocative backdrop for many 1920s films, including *Stagecoach* and *Wee Willie Winkle*.

Children's Museum of Los Angeles

818-786-2656
www.childrensmuseumla.org

Come summer of 2007, kids and parents will find this museum—which spent 21 years in Los Angeles's Civic Center—in the San Fernando Valley's beautiful Hansen Dam Recreation Park (exact address to be announced). The new facility, at some 60,000 square feet of both indoor and outdoor space, is being designed "to educate, entertain, and empower children and the adults who care for them." Exhibits in the works—about America's native peoples, health and safety, and the Earth, among many other subjects—will emphasize the value of building community. Museum officials promise innovative and environmentally friendly architecture throughout the site and plenty of hands-on, participatory activities and special events year round. For news about the museum's reopening, visit the Web site.

Chinese American Museum

425 N. Los Angeles Street, Los Angeles (Map No. 1)
213-485-8567
www.camla.org

Open: Tu–Su, 10:00 AM–3:00 PM
Recommended donation: Adults, $3.00; Seniors and Students, $2.00
Parking: Pay parking in nearby lots; also street parking

Chinese first settled in Los Angeles in the 1850s and the Garnier Building, built in 1890, was once occupied by notable Chinese American businesses and social, religious, and educational organizations. Today it stands as the last surviving structure of Old Chinatown, located in the city's original pueblo downtown. It is fitting, then, that the Garnier Building gives space to this young museum dedicated to illuminating the history of Americans of Chinese ancestry, from the earliest pioneers to the newest immigrants. On display are photographs, home videos, and a wide variety of objects—from furniture, ceramics, and books to mah jong sets and Chinese New Year parade costumes—which taken together delineate more than 150 years of Chinese immigration, struggle, achievement, and community-building in Los Angeles and beyond. Galleries on the second floor are used for temporary exhibitions about modern and contemporary Chinese American art, ideas, and issues. The Chinese American Museum is part of El Pueblo de Los Angeles Historical Monument.

Highlight:

A re-creation of a turn-of-the-century Chinese American herb shop

Chinese Historical Society of Southern California

411 and 415 Bernard Street, Los Angeles (Map No. 1)
323-222-0856
www.chssc.org

Open: W–F, 11:00 AM–3:00 PM; Su, Noon–4:30 PM
Admission: Free
Parking: Limited parking in facility lot; also pay parking in nearby lots
and street parking

For more than 30 years, this historical society has worked to
preserve, interpret, and communicate knowledge of the history
of Chinese and Chinese Americans in the region. While its
offices serve primarily as a resource center, where one can gain
access to hundreds of oral histories and other archival material,
several objects from the organization's collection of 200,000
artifacts are also usually on view. These were excavated in
1989–1991, when the Metropolitan Transit Authority was
building a new subway line at Union Station, the site of Old
Chinatown. From exquisite porcelain teacups to Asian coins to
opium pipes, these objects help to portray the everyday life of
Old Chinatown's residents before they were forcibly moved in
1934 to make way for the station. The organization also holds
approximately 10,000 artifacts from archaeological digs con-
ducted at the site of Santa Barbara's Chinatown as well as historic photographs, maps, and paintings portraying Chinese
Angeleno life.

Civil Rights Museum

10950 S. Central Avenue, Los Angeles (Map No. 1)
323-563-5600
www.wlcac.org

Open: By appointment only
Admission: Adults, $5.00; Seniors, Students, and Children under 12, $3.00
Parking: Free parking in facility lot

Operated under the auspices of the Watts Labor Community
Action Committee (WLCAC) and located in what's known
in the neighborhood as "The Center"—a seven-acre site celebrating the diverse artistic and cultural heritage of the city of
Watts—this museum presents exhibitions highlighting the
struggles for civil rights in the United States. Upon entering,
visitors will encounter a replica of the hold of a slave ship,
installed to call to mind the deplorable treatment of human
beings taken into slavery. It is filled with sculptures of human
figures by WLCAC resident artist Charles Dickson and created using body casts of local students. Within the halls of The
Center's Freedom Hall is the museum's core exhibition,
Countdown to Eternity, which centers around Martin Luther
King, Jr. and the Civil Rights Movement of the 1960s.
Included here are photographs taken by photojournalist
Benedict Fernandez during the last two years of King's life.
Other exhibitions include *1968: Black Panthers*, featuring photo-
graphs taken by Howard L. Bingham for *LIFE*, and *Hall of
Shame*, displaying racist artifacts that illuminate the state of race
relations prior to the 1960s.

Craft and Folk Art Museum

5814 Wilshire Boulevard, Los Angeles (Map No. 1)
323-937-4230
www.cafam.org

Open: W–Su, 11:00 AM–5:00 PM
Admission: Adults, $5.00; Seniors and Students, $3.00; Children under 13, Free; also, free general admission on first Wednesday of every month
Parking: Pay parking in nearby lots; also street parking.

Once known memorably as The Egg and the Eye, this museum along Wilshire Boulevard's "Museum Row" presents and preserves folk art and contemporary craft from Southern California and around the world. While the museum no longer holds a permanent collection, it is the venue for many changing exhibitions spotlighting glassware, textiles, toys, masks, and other handmade creations. One recent exhibition focused on costumes and other objects made from straw as a way to express the universal culture of the harvest; another exhibited contemporary voodoo flags, metal sculpture, and works on canvas.

Downey Museum of Art

10419 S. Rives Avenue, Downey (Map No. 1)
562-861-0419
[notable art]

Open: Call ahead for hours
Admission: Free
Parking: Free in community park's lot

This museum of contemporary art focuses on works by multi-cultural, emerging, and/or women artists in Southern California. At the core of its permanent holdings are more than 100 works by Los Angeles artist Boris Deutsch, said to comprise the largest collection of his work outside of New York City's Museum of Modern Art. Changing exhibitions come through the museum's doors throughout the year, including the recent *Traces of Identity: An Insider's View of the L.A. Armenian Community* and *Innovation/Imagination: 50 Years of Polaroid Photography*. Currently the museum is awaiting relocation and expansion, with plans to build an ecologically designed facility surrounded by a sculpture and botanical garden; call ahead for up-to-date information on this move.

Highlight:
Boris Deutsch's *Fire Eater* (1846)

Drum Barracks Civil War Museum

1052 Banning Boulevard, Wilmington (Map No. 3)
310-548-7509
www.drumbarracks.org

Open: Access to museum by hour-long guided tour only, offered on the hour Tu–Th, 10:00 AM–1:00 PM, and on the half-hour Sa–Su, 11:30 AM–2:30 PM
Admission: Adults, $3.00; Children under 12, Free
Parking: Free in museum lot

Visitors may be surprised to learn of California's involvement in the Civil War, but a trip to this museum reveals the state's role as the U.S. Army headquarters for Southern California and the Arizona Territory from 1862 through 1871. Named after Richard Coulter Drum, Assistant Adjutant General of the Department of the Pacific, the military facility protected the Wilmington Harbor and acted to secure for the Union a widely-encompassing region thought to be a hotbed for Confederate sympathizers. The museum, which preserves the history of Drum Barracks, is housed in what were the Junior Officers' Quarters, now the only U.S. Army building in the Los Angeles area that remains intact from the Civil War. Rooms are set up to reflect life at camp, with a parlor room depicting how soldiers spent their leisure time and an officer's bedroom presenting Civil War–era fashions and furnishings. The Armory displays weapons employed in the war—rifles, muskets, carbines, pistols, and bullets—along with an operable Gatling Gun, the famous early rapid-firing gun, from 1875. The research library maintains a large collection of books from the period, including a complete set of the Official Records of the

Union and Confederate Armies (accessible by appointment only, with a $5.00-per-day research fee).

Additional highlights:

An ink-printed 34-star flag, found in 1863 on the battlefield of Vicksburg, Mississippi by Private William Stephens

The only known photo of a U.S. Army camel used to carry supplies and equipment in the southwest during the Civil War

An artificial leg worn by a Civil War soldier

El Monte Historical Society Museum

3150 N. Tyler Avenue, El Monte (Map No. 4)
626-444-3813 or 626-580-2232

Open: Tu–F, 10:00 AM–4:00 PM; Su, 1:00–3:00 PM
Admission: Free; donations encouraged
Parking: Free in facility lot

Although the pioneers who would populate El Monte traveled to California in search of gold, they settled in an area rich in agricultural opportunities. Here they benefited from the water supplied by the nearby San Gabriel River, at the end of the Santa Fe Trail. This museum, which you'll find in El Monte's original public library building, celebrates the city's heritage as the oldest settlement in the San Gabriel Valley. The museum's many historical artifacts, personal belongings of residents past and present, and memorabilia are organized thematically. One exhibit shows pioneer family heirlooms, such as furniture and handmade quilts from the 1800s. Another re-creates El Monte's main street in the early 1900s, complete with replicas of the country store, pharmacy, and photo studio, which displays a movie camera from 1866, one of the first ever built and powered, of all things, by candle! The dress and hat rooms present women's clothing dating back to the city's founding through the early 1900s.

Additional highlights:

A 1911 Model T Ford, with brass kerosene cowl and tail lamps

A display about the town's famous Gay's Lion Farm, a tourist attraction from 1924 to 1941

The Erotic Museum

6741 Hollywood Boulevard, Los Angeles (Map No. 1)
323-GO-EROTIC (323-463-7684)
www.theeroticmuseum.com

Open: Su–Th, 11:00 AM–8:00 PM; F–Sa, 11:00 AM–11:00 PM
Admission: Adults, $12.95; Students and Seniors, $9.95; no one under 18 admitted
Parking: Pay parking in nearby lots; also street parking

Only the second of its kind in the United States, this museum hopes to spark fun, honest debate on the positive potential of human sexuality. To fulfill this mission, its 6,000-square-foot gallery features a range of erotic art, artifacts, and interactive exhibits, such as a Toy Box full of sexually charged objects that visitors can touch for themselves. On permanent display are two highlights of the museum's collection: a sampling of Pablo Picasso's late-career etchings of orgies and other wanton encounters and photographer Tom Kelly's "Red Velvet" nudes, which helped catapult Marilyn Monroe to sex-queen stardom. An educational, graphically illustrated timeline marks key moments in a century of sex, from the death of Queen Victoria and the invention of plastic to the X-rated films of John Holmes and the explosion of Internet pornography.

Additional highlights:

Thomas Edison's film *The Kiss* (1896), which documented a lip-locked couple to the dismay of the censors

Stairway to Hefner, showcasing personal effects of the *Playboy* king

Randy photographs by David LaChapelle and rare art books by homoeroticist Tom of Finland

The Fashion Institute of Design and Merchandise Museum and Galleries

919 S. Grand Avenue, Los Angeles (Map No. 1)

213-623-5821

www.fidm.edu/resources/museum+galleries

Open: Only during exhibitions; check Web site for exhibition schedule

Admission: Varies by exhibition; check Web site for exhibition fees

Parking: Pay parking in facility garage; also pay parking in nearby lots and street parking

While shopping in Los Angeles's 90-block fashion district, check out what's in vogue at the museum of FIDM, short for the Fashion Institute of Design and Merchandise. On the ground floor of the college is an 11,000-square-foot gallery where temporary exhibitions are mounted throughout the year. While these often bring together works from other collections (a recent exhibition, *Dressing the Galaxy*, showed off the other-worldly wardrobe of the *Star Wars* movies), FIDM holds well over 10,000 costumes, accessories, and textiles from the 18th century to the present. The label-conscious will be happy to spot top-designer apparel by the likes of Chanel and Christian Lacroix. Cinephiles, meanwhile, will enjoy the museum's annual show of costumes from the previous year's Academy Award contenders and other recent releases. As of 2006, FIDM also safeguards the collection of the Annette Green Perfume Museum, the only one in the United States to explore the heritage of fragrance and serve as a repository for industry memorabilia, such as antique and contemporary perfume bottles.

Forest Lawn Museum

1712 S. Glendale Avenue, Glendale (Map No. 2)
1-800-204-3131
www.forestlawn.com/visitors_guide/museum.asp

Open: Daily, 10:00 AM–5:00 PM
Admission: Free
Parking: Free in museum lot and throughout facility

Hubert Eaton (1881–1966), the founder of Southern California's Forest Lawn Memorial Parks, is remembered for revolutionizing the funeral industry. Pledging to rid the landscape of "unsightly, depressing stoneyards" and opting instead for rolling hills with gravestones laid flush to the ground, stately architecture, and inspiring fountains and statuary, he built final resting places reflecting his optimistic view of death. Eaton also collected an eclectic mix of art, which forms the basis of this museum located at the Glendale facility. Ancient Greek and Roman coins, 15th-century stained glass, Asian and European decorative arts, crown-jewel replicas, and several Western American–themed bronze statues are among the museum's holdings. Gallery space is also reserved for temporary exhibitions, the themes of which have varied from sacred relics to rock-album art. In a separate building, the Memorial Court of Honor, and throughout the site, there are a number of full-sized reproductions of Renaissance sculptures, including Michelangelo's *Moses* and *David*. By the way, Spencer Tracy, Nat King Cole, and Clara Bow are among the numerous celebrities interred here, but be warned that park policy forbids the staff from divulging exact locations of their graves.

Highlights:

William Bougereau's *Song of the Angels* (1881)

"Henry," the last and one of very few stone heads to be removed from Easter Island

Rosa Caselli Moretti's stained glass recreation of Leonardo da Vinci's *The Last Supper*, presented with dramatic narration every half hour

Fort MacArthur Museum

3601 S. Gaffey Street, San Pedro (Map No. 3)
310-548-2631
www.ftmac.org

Open: Tu, Th and Sa–Su, Noon–5:00 PM
Admission: Free
Parking: Free in adjacent lot

Perched high above the Pacific Ocean on 20 acres of land, this museum proudly guards the history of the U.S. Army post that protected the nation's western shores from 1914 to 1982. The fort—named in honor of Lieutenant General Arthur MacArthur, a Civil War Medal of Honor recipient and the father of General Douglas MacArthur—defended the Port of Los Angeles and the continental coastline during the world wars and later became the headquarters for the Los Angeles area air defense system. The museum's galleries are contained within the underground walls of the historic Battery Osgood-Farley, built during 1916–1919 to house two 14-inch "disappearing mount" seacoast artillery guns. Exhibits mark historic advances in coastal defense, from the big guns of the early 20th century to the NIKE missiles of the Cold War. A considerable collection of photographs, newspaper clippings, memorabilia, and military equipment conveys the eminence of Los Angeles as a military port, recounts the attack on Pearl Harbor, and addresses the pivotal role of civil defense during wartime. While at the museum, spend time in former powder and shell rooms, study a replica of an air raid house, or test out World War II–era communications tubes that run from one end of the battery to the other. Also be sure to visit lookout stations at the top of the grounds for breathtaking views of the ocean.

Frederick R. Weisman Museum of Art

24255 Pacific Coast Highway, Center for the Arts,
Pepperdine University, Malibu (Map No. 1)
310-506-4851
www.pepperdine.edu/arts/museum

Open: Tu–Su, 11:00 AM–5:00 PM; also open one hour prior to Center
for the Arts evening performances through intermission
Admission: Free
Parking: Limited free parking on campus; inquire at university information booths

The campus of Pepperdine University, hugged on one side by
the Santa Monica Mountains and the Malibu coastline on the
other, is the idyllic site of this museum, one of a few around
the country funded by the Frederick R. Weisman Art
Foundation. Established by its late namesake—the highly successful businessman who was famous for his philanthropy and
support of the visual arts—the foundation is the keeper of
Weisman's world-class collection of modern and contemporary
art. Works from here find their way into the museum from
time to time, making it a place where Pepperdine students and
visitors can view works by countless major artists represented in
the collection, including Paul Cezanne, Max Ernst, Robert
Rauschenberg, Mark Rothko, Helen Frankenthaler, Andy
Warhol, Ed Ruscha, and Nam June Paik. The museum also
hosts changing exhibitions, often focusing on California art,
and gives Pepperdine art students a chance to show their best
work during the school year.

Frederick's of Hollywood Celebrity Lingerie Museum

6608 Hollywood Boulevard, Los Angeles (Map No. 1)
323-957-5953

Open: M–F, 10:00 AM–9:00 PM; Sa, 10:00 AM–7:00 PM; Su, 11:00 AM–6:00 PM
Admission: Free
Parking: Street parking

Where else would one find a museum next to fishnets and garter belts but in the flagship store of Frederick's of Hollywood? At the back of this world-famous boutique is the cozy Celebrity Lingerie Museum, offering visitors a peep at underwear worn by some of entertainment's biggest stars. On view are peignoirs, negligees, petticoats, and other intimate apparel pulled from the closets of Loni Anderson, Greta Garbo, Cher, Zsa Zsa Gabor, and many more. After ogling the exhibits, learn more about the founder of Frederick's of Hollywood, Frederick Mellinger. Museum text panels tell of his dream to help the average American woman feel like a pin-up girl and celebrate his many innovations, including the push-up bra and thong panties.

Highlights:
Tony Curtis's bra from *Some Like It Hot*
The bustier worn by Madonna in *Who's That Girl?*

The Gamble House

4 Westmoreland Place, Pasadena (Map No. 2)
626-793-3334
www.gamblehouse.org

Open: Access to house by guided tour only, offered every 15 minutes,
Th–Su, Noon–3:00 PM
Admission: Adults, $8.00; Seniors and Students, $5.00; Children under
12, Free
Parking: Free in facility lot

With its sculptural woodwork, Tiffany glass, and one-of-a-kind
furniture, this National Historic Landmark is internationally
recognized as one of the most significant surviving examples of
Arts and Crafts architecture in the world. The talents behind
the masterpiece, a commission by David and Mary Gamble of
Procter & Gamble, were brother architects Charles and
Henry Greene. From 1907 through 1909, Greene & Greene
conceived and constructed the residence and practically all of
its furnishings. Museum guides shed light on the back-to-
nature design philosophy behind the house's distinctive features, including the use of diverse exotic woods, from Burmese
teak to birdseye maple to San Domingo mahogany; the
exposed joinery, much of it in ebony; the emphasis on the hor-
izontal, even in the tile grouting; and the faithful repetition of
shapes, patterns, and motifs such as roses, bats, and cranes.
Although most of what's on display was present when the
Gambles occupied the house, there are also a few objects that
have been gifted to the historic house's collection of period art,
such as a group of Rookwood vases and furniture by Stickley,
the only other make of furniture that Greene & Greene
allowed in the house aside from its own custom works.

The Geffen Contemporary at MOCA*

152 N. Central Avenue, Los Angeles (Map No. 1)

213-626-6222

www.moca.org

Open: Only during exhibitions—M and F, 11:00 AM–5:00 PM; Th,
11:00 AM–8:00 PM; Sa–Su, 11:00 AM–6:00 PM; check Web site for
exhibition schedule
Admission: Adults, $8.00; Seniors and Students, $5.00; Children under
12, Free; also, free general admission on Thursdays, 5:00–8:00 PM
Parking: Pay parking in nearby lots; also street parking

In 1983, acclaimed architect Frank O. Gehry transformed a
onetime police-car garage into this facility of the Museum of
Contemporary Art (MOCA), named in honor of a major gift
from the foundation of Hollywood mogul and art collector
David Geffen. Temporary shows of all genres of contemporary
art are mounted, often pulling works from MOCA's renowned
collections; see the entry about MOCA's main location, on
Grand Avenue, to learn more about these permanent holdings.

*See separate entries about the museum's other two facilities,
the Museum of Contemporary Art, Grand Avenue, and the
Museum of Contemporary Art, Pacific Design Center.

The Getty Center

1200 Getty Center Drive, Los Angeles (Map No. 1)
310-440-7300
www.getty.edu

Open: Tu–Th and Su, 10:00 AM–6:00 PM; F–Sa, 10:00 AM–9:00 PM
Admission: Free
Parking: Pay parking in museum garage

Upon his death, in 1976, oil tycoon J. Paul Getty bequeathed a
not-so-small fortune to the trust that bears his name, which
was created for "the diffusion of artistic and general knowledge." To fulfill this purpose, the trust's financial resources have
been used to create and operate a multifaceted institution
housed primarily at the Getty Center, of which the J. Paul
Getty Museum is a part. Inaugurated in 1997, the hilltop
Richard Meier–designed facility—featuring buildings clad in
glass, aluminum, and rough-hewn travertine from the same
quarry the Romans tapped to build the Colosseum—affords
plenty of space to mount changing exhibitions and to exhibit
the museum's focused collections of art. Getty's personal
acquisitions—of 18th-century French furniture, ancient Greek
and Roman art, and a select group of European paintings—lay
the groundwork for these holdings. Today the museum collects
in seven areas. Its European drawings, manuscripts, sculpture,
and decorative arts are all strictly pre-20th-century. Strengths
are in various areas—Italian Renaissance drawings,
International Style illumination, and British Neoclassical
sculpture, to name a few. The approximately 450 European
paintings, which hang in galleries bathed in natural light, are
also from before 1900; among them are Jan Steen's *The Drawing*

Lesson (1626) and Vincent van Gogh's *Irises* (1889). The museum's antiquities now live at the Getty Villa (see p. 48). Finally, the museum's extensive and renowned collection of European and American photographs, dating back to photography's experimental beginnings to the present, represents the museum's debut in 20th-century art. Expect to see the work of many great achievers in the medium, such as Gustave Le Gray, Julia Margaret Cameron, and Man Ray.

While outdoors at the Getty Center, visitor will soak up spectacular views of Meier's architecture and the city it overlooks, come upon modern sculptures gifted to the Getty by the late film producer Ray Stark, and encounter lush gardens designed by landscape architect Laurie Olin. They will also stumble upon a site-specific work of art that changes with the seasons: the Central Garden, described by its maker, artist Robert Irwin, as "a sculpture in the form of a garden aspiring to be art."

Additional highlights:

A number of works attributed to royal cabinetmaker André-Charles Boulle and his Parisian atelier

The giant *Christ's Entry into Brussels in 1889* (1888), by James Ensor

Portrait of a Halberdier (1528–1530), by Pontormo

The Stammheim Missal (ca. 1170s)

Camille Silvy's 1858 masterpiece *River Scene*

The Getty Villa

17985 Pacific Coast Highway, Pacific Palisades (Map No. 1)
310-440-7300
www.getty.edu

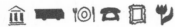

Open: Th–M, 10:00 AM–5:00 PM
Admission: Free, but advance, timed tickets required; call ahead or
visit the Web site to check availability and place ticket order
Parking: Pay parking in museum garage, available to ticketholders only

Before the Getty Center* opened, in 1997, the Getty Villa was
where visitors and Angelenos went to view the collections of
the J. Paul Getty Museum. After an eight-year renovation,
with architects Rodolfo Machado and Jorge Silvetti at the
helm, the Getty Villa has reopened its doors. Now modernized
and luxuriously reimagined is the original 1970s edifice that J.
Paul Getty had architectural firm Langdon Wilson, with guid-
ance from historian Norman Neuerburg, design and build: a
re-creation (of sorts) of the Villa dei Papiri, a first-century
Roman country home that was buried when Mt. Vesuvius
erupted in 79 CE. This is the apt setting for the museum's
trove of ancient Greek, Roman, and Etruscan art. More than
1,200 of the approximately 44,000 total holdings are on view in
galleries filled with natural light and boasting refurbished ter-
razzo floors. They are organized by theme — heroes in literature, gods and goddesses, and Dionysos and the theater, for
example. Favorites from the old Getty Villa are here, like the
Lansdowne Herakles statue, said to be one of Mr. Getty's
most prized possessions, as are more recent acquisitions, such as
the collection of ancient glass. The look and feel of antiquity
extend outdoors to the villa's four gardens, planted with trees,

herbs, and flowers used by the ancient Romans and adorned with bronze statues, sculptural fountains, and reflecting pools. While enjoying these and other lovely spots on the 64-acre grounds, you'll catch sweeping vistas of the Pacific Ocean.

*See the Getty Center entry in this volume.

Additional highlights:

Victorious Youth (300–100 BCE), one of very few surviving life-sized Greek bronzes

The Hall of Colored Marble

The hotly debated *Statue of a Kouros*, dating either to about 530 BCE or a modern forgery!

Gordon R. Howard Museum

115 Lomita Street, Burbank (Map No. 2)
818-841-6333
www.burbankhistsoc.com
Open: Sa–Su, 1:00–4:00 PM
Admission: Free; donations encouraged
Parking: Street parking

Founded in 1887, when local dentist David Burbank sold his sizeable holdings to land speculators, the town of Burbank became the San Fernando Valley's first independent city in 1911. This museum aims to preserve the history of this community over the past century. The donations of its citizens, along with several objects on indefinite loan, fill the galleries with vintage automobiles, farm equipment, Native American artifacts, period furniture, paintings of early Burbank, and much more. Also on display are the personal collections of several local residents—of dolls, miniature chairs, and model cars, to name a few. Special exhibits of memorabilia, historical photographs, and press clippings pay tribute to local heroes, including heavyweight boxing champ Jim Jeffries; the Burbank Road Kings Car Club; the Lockheed Corporation, which helped lift Burbank out of the Depression when it moved its main plant there in the mid-1930s; and the studios of Warner Bros., Walt Disney, and NBC, all of which still call Burbank home.

Grier Musser Museum

403 S. Bonnie Brae Street, Los Angeles (Map No. 1)

213-413-1814

www.griermussermuseum.com

Open: W–Sa, Noon–4:00 PM

Admission: Adults, $6.00; Seniors and Students, $5.00; Children, $4.00

Parking: LImited free parking in museum lot; also pay parking in near-by lots and street parking

The holidays set the tone at this museum located inside a restored Queen Anne–style house in downtown Los Angeles. Depending on the time of year, visitors will feast their eyes on different antiques, souvenirs, books, dolls, and assorted curios pulled from the museum's wide-ranging collections. Come around Chinese New Year to find exquisite Chinese porcelain; swing by closer to Independence Day to see Statue of Liberty memorabilia and blue and red glassware. In December, the museum decks the halls with a wealth of Christmas ornaments, Santa Claus decorations, nativity scenes, and vintage greeting cards. Other occasions and themes explored by the museum in recent years include back-to-school September, the anniversary of Hawaii's statehood, the suffrage movement, and Elvis Presley; check the Web site to find out what seasonal exhibits are coming up. The objects are showcased festively in domestic room settings and complement the house's intricate woodwork, stained glass, chandeliers, and other fine architectural details.

Highlights:

Valentine's Day cards dating back to the 1890s

Extensive holdings of *Alice in Wonderland* memorabilia

Guinness World of Records Museum

6764 Hollywood Boulevard, Los Angeles (Map No. 1)

323-463-6433

www.guinnessattractions.com

Open: Daily, 10:00 AM–Midnight

Admission: Adults, $10.95; Children 6–12, $6.95; Children under 6, Free; discounts available when purchasing tickets to both this museum and the Hollywood Wax Museum across the street.

Parking: Pay parking in nearby lots; also street parking

At this Hollywood Walk of Fame tourist attraction, experience just some of the data collected, authenticated, and publicized by the undisputed leader in world-record keeping. Interactive multimedia installations, dioramas, mannequins, photographs, and text from the pages of the *Guinness Book of World Records* illustrate hundreds of top-ranking achievements and skills. They're organized by the sorts of categories one finds in the bestselling book, such as the human body, space, and sports, and include superlatives like the world's heaviest man, the highest shallow dive survived, and the most fan mail received. Although the building's façade and overall structure are not restored to the original, the museum is housed inside the historic Hollywood Theater, which, built in 1938, was Hollywood's first movie house and is now a National Registered Landmark.

Heritage Square Museum

3800 Homer Street, Los Angeles (Map No. 1)
323-225-2700
www.heritagesquare.org

Open: Grounds only—F–Su and most holiday Mondays, Noon–5:00
PM; access to house interiors by guided tour only, offered hourly,
Noon–4:00 PM
Admission: Adults and Children 13–17, $10.00; Seniors, $8.00;
Children 6–12, $5.00; Children under 6, Free
Parking: Street parking

This museum in Highland Park has literally collected eight historic buildings, saving them from demolition over the last 30 years and transplanting them here. All were built in the late 19th century, a time when Southern California and the nation at large were witness to important advances in transportation, communications, and distribution systems. Along with modernization came a boom in housing and the rise of new, eclectic architecture throughout Los Angeles. The eight structures that stand in Heritage Square hail from this eventful era and let visitors see how Angelenos of that period lived. The Hale House, for example, with its fish-scale shingles and dentil blocks, is a classic example of the Queen Anne style. Some of its walls are covered with the leather-like lincrusta, a kind of wall covering that was very much in vogue at the time. Next door, the Perry House, Los Angeles's oldest standing mansion, is an opulent Greek Revival/Italianate residence flaunting a dining room, then a novel feature of home design. Also on view are an Eastlake-style train depot that once served the Southern Pacific Railroad and the eight-sided Longfellow-

Hastings Octagonal House, designed along the theories of Orson S. Fowler, who argued that an eight-sided structure costs less to build and makes for better air flow. The buildings are in various stages of restoration, so every visit to the museum may reveal new aspects of the buildings and deeper insight into the lives of those who used them.

Hermosa Beach Historical Society Museum

710 Pier Avenue, Hermosa Beach (Map No. 3)
310-318-9421
www.hermosabeachhistoricalsociety.org

Open: Sa–Su, 2:00–4:00 PM
Admission: Free
Parking: Free in facility lot

A hundred years ago, Hermosa Beach, which stretches along two miles of white sandy coastline, was a resort destination for Angelenos craving sun and sand. Today it lives on as a quaint city with the beach as its playground. Tucked inside the city's busy community center, this museum of photographs, documents, memorabilia, and residents' personal treasures traces the history of Hermosa Beach's schools, library, pier, and boardwalk, and takes a fun look at beach volleyball, a thriving Hermosa Beach pastime since the 1920s. Exhibits underscoring the importance of the town's entertainment venues are also mounted, featuring a playbill from its first theater, a nickelodeon named the Hermosa Theatre, as well as original seats and marquee letters from the Bijou Theater, built in 1923. Expansion of the museum is underway, with plans to feature theme rooms highlighting Hermosa Beach's early history, city growth and development, recreational life, and some of the people who have shaped the cozy oceanside community.

Hollyhock House

4800 Hollywood Boulevard, Los Angeles (Map No. 1)

323-644-6269

www.hollyhockhouse.net

Open: Access to house by guided tour only, offered hourly, W–Su,
12:30–3:30 PM

Admission: Adults, $5.00; Seniors and Students, $3.00; Children under
12, Free

Parking: Free in Barnsdall Park lot; also street parking

When oil heiress and theater lover Aline Barnsdall decided to
build an arts commune in Los Angeles, she turned to Frank
Lloyd Wright. His plan called for several structures, most of
which were to serve the artists in residence, but growing differ-
ences between client and architect limited construction to this
now-famous house along with two secondary dwellings. Built
between 1919 and 1923, the house was Wright's first project in
Los Angeles and thus represents his earliest architectural
response to the climate and culture of the region, a style he
called California Romanza. Noteworthy features include a
moat surrounding the living room fireplace; glass corners in
several rooms; ornamental details inspired by the hollyhock,
Barnsdall's favorite flower; and a floor plan by which every
interior space has an adjoining outdoor space to match. The
house also contains what may well be the first built-in entertainment center, with cabinets sized perfectly for LPs. The
Hollyhock House is part of the 35-acre Barnsdall Park, where
visitors will also find a municipal art gallery, art studios, and a
theater. Art shows are occasionally mounted inside the house;
check the Web site for the schedule of exhibitions.

Hollywood Bowl Museum

2301 N. Highland Avenue, Los Angeles (Map No. 1)
323-850-2058
www.hollywoodbowl.org/event/museum.cfm

Open: During concert season (July–mid September), Tu–Sa, 10:00
AM–show time, and Su, 4:00 PM–show time; during concert off-sea-
son, Tu–Sa, 10:00 AM–4:30 PM
Admission: Free
Parking: Free parking in facility lot before 4:30 PM; otherwise, pay
parking in facility and nearby lots; also very limited street parking

The Rolling Stones. Barbra Streisand. Van Cliburn.
Radiohead.— For more than 80 years, the best in music have
performed live at the beloved performing arts facility known as
the Hollywood Bowl. Since its humble beginnings in 1920,
when community events were staged on a plain wooden plat-
form in the canyon recognized for its acoustic excellence, the
open-air theater has welcomed hundreds of thousands of artists
and concertgoers season after season. At its on-site museum,
the story of the Bowl is told through letters, programs, photographs, artifacts, and more. Included in this nostalgic look at
the venue's history are the origins of the popular Easter Sunrise
Service; the Bowl's longtime relationship with the Los Angeles
Philharmonic; the benefit concerts mounted to aid wounded
World War II soldiers; and the pandemonium rising from the
sold-out shows by the Beatles in 1964 and 1965. Slip on head-
phones at audio stations throughout the museum's main gallery
and hear sound clips from key Hollywood Bowl recordings.

Highlights:

The RCA 77 microphone used in 1943 by Frank Sinatra, the first pop-music performer to take the stage at the Hollywood Bowl

Architectural models tracing the evolving design of the Hollywood Bowl stage, especially its iconic Moderne "shell" of sleek concentric arches

Clips from movies featuring the Hollywood Bowl, from *A Star Is Born* to *Beaches*

Hollywood Entertainment Museum

7021 Hollywood Boulevard, Los Angeles (Map No. 1)

323-465-7900

www.hollywoodmuseum.com

Open: Labor Day through Memorial Day, daily except Wednesday, 11:00 AM–6:00 PM; Memorial Day through Labor Day, daily, 10:00 AM–6:00 PM

Admission: Adults, $12.00; Seniors, $10.00; Students, $5.00; Children under 6, Free

Parking: Pay parking with museum validation in facility garage and in nearby lots; also street parking

While reading celebrity names in the star-studded sidewalk of the Hollywood Walk of Fame, stop into this interactive destination. Offering a behind-the-scenes look at what the museum triumphantly calls "the stuff that dreams are made of," the museum shows what can be found on a studio backlot. The simulated property and wardrobe departments are packed with props and costumes from both film and television, such as armor worn in *Ben Hur*. The visitor experience culminates in a tour of the original stage sets of the bridge from *Star Trek: The Next Generation*, the *Cheers* bar, and Special Agent Fox Mulder's office from *The X-Files*. Feel free to sit in Norm's well-worn bar stool—the museum encourages it! The museum also boasts a number of vintage cameras, projectors, televisions, and other historically significant hardware used in entertainment technology.

Highlights:

A simulated Foley room in which visitors can try creating sound effects and synchronizing them to a video clip

The Max Factor Collection of cosmetic products and tools

The piano from the Masquers Bar, the distinguished Hollywood theatrical club (active 1925–2002), signed by such members as Cary Grant and Buster Keaton

Hollywood Heritage Museum

2100 N. Highland Avenue, Los Angeles (Map No. 1)

323-874-4005

www.hollywoodheritage.org

Open: Sa–Su, 11:00 AM–4:00 PM

Admission: Adults, $6.00; Seniors and Students, $3.00; Children 3–12, $1.00; Children under 3, Free

Parking: Free in museum lot

In 1913, a young, rising director named Cecil B. DeMille, along with business partner Jesse Lasky, rented half of a simple wood-frame barn located in the heart of Hollywood for use as a studio (a stable of horses occupied the other half, at least at first). It was here, later that year, that DeMille shot the first feature-length film ever made in Hollywood, the box-office hit *The Squaw Man*, making the so-called Lasky-DeMille Barn the birthplace of Hollywood's motion picture industry. Today the structure is home to this museum, which displays an assortment of archival photographs, props, screenplays, posters, and other historic movie memorabilia. Visitors not only trace the history of early Hollywood filmmaking, in particular how Lasky, DeMille, and other leaders launched Paramount Studios, but also the architectural development of Hollywood—both residential and commercial—during its heyday.

Highlights:

Three rare, authentic handmade box cameras

A recreation of DeMille's private office, featuring period furniture and the filmmaker's glasses, shoes, and riding crop

Spears, shields, and armor from DeMille classics *The Ten Commandments* and *The Crusades*

The Hollywood Museum

1660 N. Highland Avenue, Los Angeles (Map No. 1)
323-464-7776
www.thehollywoodmuseum.com

Open: Th–Su, 10:00 AM–5:00 PM
Admission: Adults, $15.00; Seniors and Children under 12, $12.00
Parking: Pay parking in adjacent lot, discounted with museum valida-
tion

The historic art deco Max Factor building, the onetime headquarters of the world-famous make-up empire, is where you'll
find this museum showcasing "motion-picture magic." The
museum's extensive collection is packed into four floors' worth
of exhibits. *Moulin Rouge*, *Planet of the Apes*, *Pee Wee's Big
Adventure*, and *Master and Commander* are just a handful of the
movies whose sets, props, and costumes can be viewed here.
The personal belongings of some of Tinseltown's biggest stars
are also on display, such as Mae West's opera glasses and Cary
Grant's 1965 Rolls Royce, as are thousands of vintage photographs, classic posters, autographs, and lobby cards. Walk
down to the basement for an eerie visit onto the original stage
set of Hannibal Lecter's prison cell. Finally, stop to appreciate
the building's splendidly restored grand salon — complete with
white marble floors, 24-carat gold and silver leaf detail, and
bas-relief ornamentation — where beauty-products master Max
Factor once catered to socialites and starlets in a glamorous
world of wigs and cosmetics.

Highlights:

Roddy McDowell's powder room, where many a celebrity
have reportedly spent time during one of his soirees

The Technicolor three-strip motion camera used to film *Gone with the Wind* and *The Wizard of Oz*

Tributes to Marilyn Monroe and Bob Hope

Hollywood Wax Museum

6767 Hollywood Boulevard, Los Angeles (Map No. 1)
323-462-8860
www.hollywoodwax.com

Open: Daily, 10:00 AM–Midnight
Admission: Adults, $12.95; Seniors, $8.50; Children 6–12, $6.95;
Children under 6, Free; discounts available when purchasing tickets to
both this museum and the Guinness World of Records Museum across
the street.
Parking: Pay parking in nearby lots; also street parking

More than 160 stars of film, television, sports, and comic
books bask in the spotlight in this house of wax, one of several
tourist attractions on Hollywood Boulevard. Get close to
some of the big and little screens' most memorable characters—from Butch Cassidy to Lara Croft, Major "Hotlips"
Houlihan to Jerry Seinfeld—as re-created by masters of wax
sculpture, make-up, hair styling, wardrobe, and set design. Also
pay your respects to pop icons like Elvis and Marilyn as well as
celebrity athletes and superheroes. Displays and figures are reg-
ularly updated to keep up with who's who and what's what in
the industry.

Highlights:

Chamber of Horrors

Three-figure display of Arnold Schwarzenegger as Conan the
Barbarian, the Terminator, and the Governor of California

The Huntington Library, Art Collections, and Botanical Gardens

1151 Oxford Road, San Marino (Map No. 4)

626-405-2100

www.huntington.org

Open: During summer (June–August), Tu–Su, 10:30 AM–4:30 PM; otherwise, Tu–F, Noon–4:30 PM and Sa–Su, 10:30 AM–4:30 PM

Admission: Adults, $15.00; Seniors, $12.00; Students, $10.00; Children 5–11, $6.00; Children under 5, Free; also, free general admission on first Thursday of every month

Parking: Free in museum lot

American railroad pioneer, utilities magnate, and real estate developer Henry Edwards Huntington (1850–1927)—together with his wife, Arabella Duval Huntington—amassed one of their generation's most prominent collections of rare books and manuscripts, fine art, and plant specimens from around the world. Today their interests live on in this educational institution, established by the couple in 1919 and set upon 120 acres of their sprawling San Marino estate. Scholars, particularly of British and American history and literature, flock to the Huntington Library (numbering about six million items) to conduct advanced research in the humanities, while the general public can experience some of the library's greatest treasures in its exhibition halls. Preeminent among these is the Ellesmere manuscript of Geoffrey Chaucer's *The Canterbury Tales* (c. 1410). The Huntington's collection of 18th- and 19th-century British and French art encompasses oil paintings, drawings, watercolors, sculpture, tapestries, furniture, porcelain, and silver. Many of these—including Thomas Gainsborough's masterpiece *The Blue Boy* (c. 1770)—are usually on view in the Myron Hunt–designed Beaux Arts mansion where Mr. and Mrs. Huntington lived. The historic structure is now closed for renovation; consult the Web site for news about its reopening. In the meantime, the European body of work is installed in a recently inaugurated gallery that will ultimately provide more room for the Huntington's growing collection of American art. Painters John Singer Sargent, Edward Hopper, and Mary Cassatt, as well as architects Charles and Henry Greene, are among the featured artists in the American collection. A group of Renaissance paintings hangs in the west wing of the library.

No trip to the Huntington would be complete without a leisurely stroll on the grounds, where more than 14,000 species of plants thrive. Twelve thematic botanical gardens—the 12-acre Desert Garden and the tranquil Japanese Garden, to name a few—present broad color palettes and widely varying ambiences. A new children's science center offers hands-on learning about plant biodiversity. Also located on the property is a mausoleum where the Huntingtons are buried. If it looks familiar, it's because its designer, John Russell Pope, used it as a model for Washington, DC's Jefferson Memorial.

Additional highlights:

Sir Thomas Lawrence's *Pinkie* (1794)

Rogier van der Weyden's *Madonna and Child* (15th century)

Extensive archives of the history of the American West

The double-elephant folio edition of John James Audubon's *Birds of America*

The Rose Garden Tea Room

International Printing Museum

315 Torrance Boulevard, Carson (Map No. 3)

310-515-7166

www.printmuseum.org

Open: Sa, 1:00–4:00 PM, or by appointment

Admission: $8.00 (includes fee for recommended guided tour)

Parking: Free in adjacent lot

At the heart of this museum prizing "mankind's single greatest invention — the printed word" is the Ernest A. Lindner Collection of Antique Printing Machinery, recognized as among the finest in the world and spanning more than 500 years of printing history. Through these notable holdings, the museum studies and interprets the development of printing and bookmaking technologies. On view are some of the many machines and tools used in written communications over the centuries, including historic wooden presses, one of the first four-color printing presses, and an exhibit detailing the invention of the linotype machine, a miracle of speed and efficiency, which eliminated the tedium of setting characters by hand. Using a replica of the Gutenberg press, docents demonstrate how the Gutenberg Bible was produced, as well as how Chinese printing blocks work. Be sure to check the schedule for actor presentations on the Constitutional Convention and on the life and legacy of founding father, printer, and publisher Benjamin Franklin.

Additional highlights:

Operational linotype machine used by the *Los Angeles Times* from 1910–1974

Ornate 1824 Columbian press, adorned in 22-carat gold leaf

Japanese American National Museum

369 E. First Street, Los Angeles (Map No. 1)
213-625-0414
www.janm.org

Open: Tu–W and F–Su, 10:00 AM–5:00 PM; Th, 10:00 AM–8:00 PM
Admission: Adults, $8.00; Seniors, $5.00; Students and Children
6–17, $4; Children under 6, Free; also, free general admission on
Thursdays, 5:00–8:00 PM, and all day on third Thursday of every
month
Parking: Pay parking in nearby lots; also street parking

Japanese Americans comprise one of the most established,
vibrant communities in California. This museum, located in
downtown Los Angeles's Little Tokyo Historic District, is the
only one in the United States designed to share the experiences
of Americans of Japanese ancestry—from initial immigration
in the late 1800s to the unconstitutional incarceration of
Japanese Americans during World War II to the present. In its
core exhibition, *Common Ground: The Heart of Community*,
hundreds of personal effects, documents, photographs, works
of art, and home movies chronicle this history, hoping to add
dimension to the meaning of ethnic and cultural diversity in
American society at large. In a poignant gesture of preserving
the memory of each individual, exhibition labels identify by full
name the person whose image and/or belongings are on display.
Those wishing to delve deeper into Japanese American refer-
ence and archival materials should also visit the museum's
Hirasaki National Resource Center.

Highlights:

Glass cases containing soil samples and artifacts from the 10 internment camps

The rebuilt authentic walls of two barracks from Heart Mountain internment camp

Uniforms, medals, and other artifacts from the service of Japanese in the U.S. military

Justice Brothers Racing Museum

2734 E. Huntington Drive, Duarte (Map No. 4)
626-359-9174
www.justicebrothers.com

Open: M–F, 8:00 AM–5:00 PM
Admission: Free
Parking: Free in facility lot

Car enthusiasts can trace the evolution of motor sports at the global headquarters of Justice Brothers, Inc., a world leader in car-care products, in particular its high-performance engine additives. In the lobby and first floor of its corporate offices (located, by the way, on the legendary Route 66) resides this museum, established in 1985 to upkeep and showcase the company's acclaimed collection of racing vehicles. Its holdings include beautifully restored circle-track race cars, ice-racing motorcycles, street rods, and dragsters, in addition to historic engines, model cars, and antique gas pumps. But the museum is about more than these gleaming works of aluminum and steel. Behind them is the success story of brothers Ed, Zeke, and Gus Justice. Long before the business that bears their name became what it is today, these three Kansas natives started out building race cars, including the winning car of the 1950 Indianapolis 500, which took the checkered flag with driving legend Johnny Parsons at the wheel.

Highlights:

A wide array of midget cars from the 1930s, 1940s, and 1950s

Two of the Indianapolis 500 racecars featured in *Driven*, starring Sylvester Stallone

Kenneth G. Fiske Museum of the Claremont Colleges

450 N. College Way, Claremont (Map No. 4)
909-621-8307
www.cuc.claremont.edu/fiske

Open: By appointment only
Admission: Free
Parking: Free in campus lots; also street parking

Caring for one of the most diverse collections of musical instruments in the country, this university museum holds more than 1,400 objects. American and European brass instruments, including rare models of cornets, trumpets, and tubas, are well represented. A select group of pianos, reed organs, and wood-wind instruments is on view, along with notable objects from the violin and viol families. There are traditional wind, string, and percussion instruments from South America, Africa, and Asia, as well as many finely decorated Tibetan trumpets. Visitors will also see one of the earliest documented pianos to have been present in the United States during the 18th century.

Highlight:

The only known complete set of seven over-the-shoulder sax-horns (1872) designed by Boston brass makers David C. Hall and Benjamin F. Quinby

Kidspace Children's Museum

480 N. Arroyo Boulevard, Pasadena (Map No. 2)
626-449-9144
www.kidspacemuseum.org

Open: Daily, 9:30 AM–5:00 PM; outdoor environments close at 4:30 PM
Admission: Adults and Children 1 and up, $8.00; Children under 1, Free
Parking: Free in museum lot

Living up to its name, this museum, just down the road from the Rose Bowl, gives children, families, caregivers, and educators a dedicated place to explore and investigate. Its learning environments invite visitors to literally touch upon the sciences and arts. Among many activities, visitors can scramble up a 40-foot "Raindrop Climber," sink their hands into a simulated paleontology dig, or try on costume mandibles in order to learn how bugs grab food. Outdoor installations include a kid-size rock-climbing wall that teaches Earth's strata formations and "Trike Tracks" for three-wheeling cyclists under 48-inches tall. The early childhood learning center provides plenty of mats, balls, mini slides, books, and other equipment to keep the littlest ones in your family busy and safe. There's a lot of water to play in, so bring swimsuits and waterproof footwear.

Additional highlights:

Exhibits teaching the geology behind and emergency preparedness for earthquakes (this is California after all!)

An interpretive arroyo, featuring a manmade stream where visitors wade their way through stones, gravel, animal models, and fossils

Korean American Museum

3727 W. 6th Street, Suite 400, Los Angeles
213-388-4229
www.kamuseum.org (Map No. 1)

Open: M–F, 11:00 AM–6:00 PM; Sa, 11:00 AM–3:00 PM
Admission: Free
Parking: Street parking

The largest community of Korean Americans calls Los
Angeles home, and this museum preserves and interprets its
history and culture. Through exhibitions—which occasionally
draw from the museum's small collection of documentary photographs—as well as lectures and forums, the museum illustrates the journey of Korean immigrants to the United States
and celebrates their unique experiences and achievements in all
facets of contemporary life. The goal is to stimulate thought
and action about the future of this thriving American community. One recent exhibition examined the explosive growth of
Los Angeles's Koreatown, while another brought forward new
work by leading Korean American artists.

Korean Cultural Center

5505 Wilshire Boulevard, Los Angeles (Map No. 1)
323-936-7141
www.kccla.org

Open: M–F, 9:00 AM–5:00 PM; Sa, 10:00 AM–1:00 PM
Admission: Free
Parking: Free in facility lot

Korea's cultural heritage spanning five millennia are the focus of this facility. In addition to providing a venue for research, performing arts, films, lectures, language classes, and monthly tea ceremonies, the center maintains a museum of historical artifacts and contemporary crafts. These give insight into Korean life throughout the centuries, especially the various dynastic periods from which several of the objects hail. For example, there are fifth- and sixth-century earthenware objects from the Silla Kingdom and examples of 12th-century *cheongja*, a blue-green porcelain that was the specialty of Goreyo Kingdom ceramicists. Also exhibited are musical instruments and ceremonial dress, as well as woodblock printing tools in honor of Korea's longstanding printing tradition. On the second floor of the center is gallery space for temporary exhibitions.

Highlights:

Jade and gold royal headgear excavated from an ancient Silla tomb

Full-scale replicas of the stone carvings of bodhisattvas found at the Seokguram Buddhist Grotto Temple in Gyeongju

Nam June Paik's *Scott Joplin as the First Digital Composer*

L. Ron Hubbard Life Exhibition

6331 Hollywood Boulevard, Los Angeles (Map No. 1)
323-960-3511
www.lronhubbardprofile.org/exhib5.htm

Open: Access to museum by guided tour only, offered every 15 minutes daily, 10:30 AM–10:00 PM
Admission: Adults and Children 12–18, $5.00; Seniors, $3.00; Children under 12, Free
Parking: Pay parking in nearby lots; also street parking

Big-time celebrities who have espoused its teachings have given the Church of Scientology a certain star power. To learn about the man who started it all, L. Ron Hubbard (1911–1986), visit this museum, where his life and legacy are exalted in more than 30 multimedia exhibits. These profile Hubbard as a pulp-fiction writer, philosopher, educator, artist, daredevil pilot, master mariner, world explorer, and, of course, the father of Scientology. On display are Hubbard's travel diaries, ceremonial objects of the Blackfoot Indians—to whom Hubbard became a blood brother—and the original typescript of his science-fiction classic *Battlefield Earth*. Visitors will be introduced to the fundamentals of Scientology, including the techniques for alleviating spiritual trauma described in Hubbard's global bestseller *Dianetics*. The museum is located inside the Hollywood Guaranty Building, a 1923 Beaux Arts–style building on the National Register of Historic Places, where Charlie Chaplin and Cecil B. De Mille once had offices.

Highlight:
A hands-on chance to try the electropsychometer, the device Scientologists use to measure thought

La Historia Society Museum/Museo de Los Barrios

3240 Tyler Avenue, El Monte (Map No. 4)
626-279-1954
www.lahistoriasociety.com

Open: Tu–Th and Sa, 11:00 AM–3:00 PM; Su, 1:00–4:00 PM
Admission: Free
Parking: Free parking in nearby lots and street parking

In 1910, the Mexican Revolution compelled hordes of families to flee northward to the United States and many were drawn to the agricultural industry of greater El Monte. Their onetime minor settlements evolved into the nine barrios of the region: Canta Ranas, Chino Camp, Hicks' Camp, La Granada, Medina Court, Las Flores, La Sección, La Misión, and Wiggins' Camp. At this museum, more than 650 photographs and documents tell the story of Mexican Americans living in the barrios from the 1920s through the early 1970s when the last one dissolved. Images depict residents at work and at play in the old neighborhoods, whether at church, school, fiesta gatherings, recreation centers, or local shops. One display pays respect to Monsignor John V. Coffield, whose efforts led to desegregation in area schools in 1945. Another section honors decades of military service by men and women from the region, from World War II to present-day Iraq. Plans to build a larger, permanent facility are underway; check the Web site for updates.

Lomita Railroad Museum

2137 W. 250th Street, Lomita (Map No. 3)
310-326-6255
www.lomita-rr.org

Open: Th–Su, 10:00 AM–5:00 PM
Admission: Adults, $4.00; Children under 12, $2.00
Parking: Free in museum lot

Mighty steam train locomotives ruled the railways from
approximately 1850 through the 1940s. This museum is dedicated to preserving this era of America's history. It was built, in
1966, to resemble Boston & Maine's Greenwood Station in
Wakefield, Massachusetts and so, upon entering, visitors may
feel as if they are stepping into a bustling turn-of-the-century
train depot. Display cases present an array of artifacts and
memorabilia relating to locomotive history and culture, including steam-train equipment and parts, lights and signals, and
communication devices used on the tracks before modernization. Also on view are items reflecting life aboard a train, such
as conductor records, waybills, tickets, a long waiting room
bench with iron armrests, and books that passengers back then
may have been reading. Visitors should wander to the adjacent
park area, where one can climb into several real-life locomotives, including a Southern Pacific Railroad Steam Locomotive
(active 1902–1960) and a 1910 Union Pacific Caboose.

Long Beach Museum of Art

2300 E. Ocean Boulevard, Long Beach (Map No. 3)
562-439-2119
www.lbma.org

Open: Tu–Sa, 11:00 AM–5:00 PM
Admission: Adults, $7.00; Seniors and Students, $6.00; Children under 12, Free; also, free general admission on Fridays
Parking: Free parking in museum lot; also street parking

Overlooking the Long Beach Harbor and the seemingly infinite blue of the Pacific Ocean, this museum's natural aesthetics are a gorgeous backdrop for the art on view. A newly constructed pavilion with two floors of gallery space is the venue for the museum's changing exhibitions. In its permanent collection are approximately 5,000 paintings, drawings, sculptures, and decorative-arts objects; select works make their way into the galleries when space permits. Of particular strength in the collection are 300 years of American decorative arts, early 20th-century European painting, California Modernism, and contemporary media and video art. Be sure to spend some time exploring the grounds, encompassing the historic 1912 Elizabeth Milbank Anderson mansion and carriage house, which now contain the museum shop and café. This pleasant setting comes complete with oceanfront gardens, an outdoor terrace, and a water sculpture by artist Claire Falkenstein.

Highlight:

California Landscapes, featuring works by George Henry Melcher (1881–1957)

Los Angeles County Museum of Art

5905 Wilshire Boulevard, Los Angeles (Map No. 1)

323-857-6000

www.lacma.org

Open: M–Tu and Th, Noon–8:00 PM; F, Noon–9:00 PM; Sa–Su, 11:00 AM–8:00 PM

Admission: Adults, $9.00; Seniors and Students, $5.00; Children under 18, Free; also, free general admission daily after 5:00 PM and all day on second Tuesday of every month

Parking: During construction (see below), none available on-site; instead, pay parking in nearby lots and street parking

More than 110,000 works of art belong to this county institution, the largest encyclopedic visual arts museum in the western United States. From Near Eastern antiquities to Dutch masterpieces, Hindu sculpture to the latest by artists on the cutting edge, the holdings of "LACMA," as it is known around town, span a staggeringly wide range of art history. Traditional Western art is in abundance, with works from ancient Greece and Rome, European painting and sculpture over the centuries, and art of the United States from colonial times to World War II. The Latin American art collection, one of the largest in the nation, is grounded in Mexican modernism. Pre-Columbian Mexican ceramics are at the core of the museum's collection of ancient American art. The diverse arts of Africa are well represented, as are the arts of Asia, encompassing China, Korea, and South and Southeast Asia. Japanese art dating back to 3000 BCE is housed in its own pavilion, designed by architect Bruce Goff and which visitors should be sure to visit. Of particular renown is the collection of Islamic art, numbering more than 1,700 works and representing 1,400 years of Islamic artistic production across Europe to Central Asia. Rounding out the collections are: works created between 1945 and the present and now encompassing newer media such as video and film; Egyptian art from over four millennia; the art of René Magritte and Henri Matisse, among other modern masters; more than 6,000 photographs; a costume and textiles collection of significant depth and breadth; medieval to contemporary decorative arts; and some 30,000 prints and drawings, especially by Southern California artists from the 1960s onward.

In 2004, LACMA selected famed architect Renzo Piano to spearhead a physical transformation of its multi-building facility. It will result in, among many other enhancements, additional and improved venues for exhibiting the permanent collection and changing exhibitions and for presenting related programs. There will be an innovative façade to unify all of LACMA's buildings, both old and new. The museum will remain open during the overhaul, set for completion in late 2007, although collections will be stored away or relocated and galleries roped off from time to time. Check the Web site for information about temporary closures and other news that may affect your visit.

Additional highlights:

The Robert Gore Rifkind Center for German Expressionist Studies

One of the most comprehensive Sri Lankan art collections outside of Asia

Mary Cassatt's *Mother About to Wash Her Sleepy Child* (1880)

Diego Rivera's *Flower Day* (1925)

The Ardabil carpet (1539–1540)

Los Angeles Fire Department Museum

1355 N. Cahuenga Boulevard, Los Angeles (Map No. 1)
323-464-2727
www.lafdhs.com

Open: Sa, 10:00 AM–4:00 PM
Admission: Free; donations encouraged
Parking: Street parking

This museum aims to preserve the history of the Los Angeles Fire Department (LAFD) and promote fire safety. Located in the fully restored, 20,000-square foot Fire Station #27, once the largest fire station west of the Mississippi, the museum holds a collection of LAFD vehicles, firefighting apparatus, historical photographs and paintings, and memorabilia spanning the many years since the department's founding, in 1886. Examples of both horse-drawn and motorized rigs are parked inside the station, complete with ladders, hoses, pumps, nozzles, valves, and the wide range of equipment used to save lives and property. Emphasis is placed on the technological and procedural advancements in firefighting throughout history. Display cases exhibit helmets, extinguishers, firefighter badges and uniforms, LAFD manuals, Smokey the Bear educational toys, and a large collection of miniature fire trucks. Although visitors can't slide down any fire poles, the site reveals the typical layout of a fire station, from offices to dormitories.

Los Angeles Live Steamers Railroad Museum

5202 Zoo Drive, Griffith Park, Los Angeles (Map No. 2)
323-662-8030
www.lals.org

Open: Su, 11:00 AM–3:00 PM, weather permitting only; Walt Disney's Barn open only on third Sunday of every month, 11:00 AM–3:00 PM
Admission: Free; passengers must be at least 34" tall
Parking: Free in museum lots; also street parking

"All aboard!" at this outdoor destination in Griffith Park, where 1/8-scale miniature trains take passengers along some 1 1/2 miles of steel-rail track. Whether by steam, electric, or diesel locomotive, you'll whiz by an entire world created in miniature, including three old-fashioned towns, two water towers, a coal tipple, even a graveyard. The railroad features a steel and truss bridge called the O'Brien-Moore Bridge, as well as three concrete tunnels measuring 112 feet combined. A fully automatic electronic signal system along with more than 80 switches make sure all the trains run safely and efficiently. During your ride, you'll pass three life-size, historic steel cabooses and a baggage dorm car built by Pullman Standard for Union Pacific in 1941. Also on the museum grounds is a red barn that once stood along Walt Disney's own miniature railroad; inside you'll find Disney's personal railroad memorabilia on display.

Los Angeles Maritime Museum

Berth 84, Foot of 6th Street, San Pedro (Map No. 2)

310-548-7618

www.lamaritimemuseum.org

Open: Tu–Sa, 10:00 AM–5:00 PM (last entry at 4:30 PM); Su,
12:00–5:00 PM (last entry at 4:30 PM)

Admission: Adults, $3.00; Seniors and Children 7–18, $1.00; Children
under 7, Free

Parking: Free in museum lot

Seafaring comes alive at this museum, which salutes the nautical
heritage of the Port of Los Angeles and coastal California. It
resides in San Pedro's original municipal ferry building, used
from 1941 to 1963 to transport cars, trucks, and thousands of
workers each day to the fishing canneries, military bases, and
shipyards located on adjacent Terminal Island. Today the former
pedestrian ramp leading to the ferry is the venue for a display of
model ships, along with a pictorial history of the harbor. Also
on view are crafts made by sailors and other maritime artifacts
and memorabilia. Upstairs, a fully operational radio station lets
visitors tune in as amateur operators, known as "hams," communicate around the globe. Be sure to walk over to the building's back deck or the three-story-tall waterside windows.
From these vantage points, visitors can observe massive ships
carrying cargo, passengers, petroleum, and much more travel in
and out of the Port of Los Angeles, one of the busiest and
most prosperous in the world.

Highlights:

A sailor-made large anchor made entirely of human hair

Information on how to build a model ship inside a bottle

Los Angeles Museum of the Holocaust

6435 Wilshire Boulevard, Ground Floor, Los Angeles (Map No. 1)

323-651-3704

www.lamuseumoftheholocaust.org

Open: M–Th, 10:00 AM–4:00 PM; F, 10:00 AM–2:00 PM; Sunday by appointment only

Admission: Free; donations encouraged

Parking: Pay parking in nearby lots; also street parking

Survivors of the Holocaust founded this museum to memorialize the approximately six million Jews exterminated by the Nazi regime and to educate the public about this dark episode in world history (1933–1945). Near the entrance, a homey display of photographs, books, clothes, sheet music, silverware, decorative objects, and toys—alongside several religious antiques—gives visitors a sense of Jewish life and times in pre-war Europe. From here, visitors follow the chain of events that gave rise to and constituted the Holocaust—Kristallnacht and the Wannsee Conference, to name just two—as well as topics relating to this history, such as the myth of racial purity, the position of the Vatican, U.S. war policy, and the call to establish a Jewish homeland. Museum text panels are complemented by relevant artifacts, photographs, and documents on display, such as the certificate revoking a certain Samuel Rapaport's German citizenship as authorized by the Nuremberg Laws; a 1945 poster giving tips on how to identify the physical traits of Jewish as distinct from Aryan youth; correspondence detailing the squalid conditions inside the Jewish ghettos; and a concentration camp uniform, hanging in one of several dimly-lit rooms filled with chilling images of those who lived and died in the Nazi death camps.

Highlights:

Original fragments of Eli Leskley's "Ghetto Diary," containing his satiric, incriminating watercolors about Jewish inmate life at Theresienstadt

A scale model of the Sobibor death camp

Yellow Star of David identification badges from several countries

Los Angeles Police Museum

6045 York Boulevard, Los Angeles (Map No. 1)

323-344-9445

www.laphs.com

Open: M–F, 10:00 AM–4:00 PM; third Saturday of every month, 9:00 AM–3:00 PM

Admission: Adults, $5.00; Seniors, $4.00; Children under 13, Free

Parking: Free in museum lot; also street parking

The Los Angeles Police Department, or LAPD, is about as sizeable and busy as a local law enforcement body can be. Since its establishment, in 1869, its efforts "To Protect and To Serve" (as goes the LAPD's official motto) the sprawling metropolis and its multitudes of citizens have made for a colorful history. This museum, operated by the Los Angeles Police Historical Society, takes visitors inside the high-profile organization, maintaining a collection of photographs, uniforms, vehicles, sirens, guns, batons, surveillance equipment, shackles, bomb squad gear, training manuals, and much more. These items hailing from different points in the LAPD's years of service are displayed to show how the police have aimed to maintain order, prevent crime, and enhance public safety throughout Los Angeles. The museum is situated inside the former Highland Park Police Station No. 11 (built in 1925), with rusty jail cells intact.

Highlights:

A tribute to women in the LAPD, or "Ladies in Blue"

Vintage merchandise from the television series *Dragnet* and *Adam-12*

MAK Center for Art and Architecture

835 N. Kings Road, West Hollywood (Map No. 1)
323-651-1510
www.makcenter.org

Open: W–Su, 11:00 AM–6:00 PM
Admission: Adults, $7.00; Seniors and Students, $6.00; Children under
12, Free; also, free general admission on Fridays, 4:00–6:00 PM, and
on Schindler's birthday, September 10
Parking: Street parking

The Schindler House is the landmark home of this institution,
run jointly by Vienna's MAK/Austrian Museum of Applied
Arts and the Friends of the Schindler House. Conceived and
built in 1922 by Austrian émigré and distinguished modern
architect Rudolph M. Schindler, the single-story, flat-roofed
dwelling is internationally recognized as one of the most daring
and influential designs of the 20th century. Its live/work floor
plan innovatively accommodates four interlocking studios laid
out in two L-shapes, seven fireplaces, and a series of outdoor
rooms defined by hedges and changes in ground level.
According to Schindler himself, the structure introduced "the
vocabulary of the modern California house." While circulating
throughout the building, imagine the salons Schindler and his
wife, Pauline, once hosted there, welcoming such esteemed cultural figures as Frank Lloyd Wright and Edward Weston. The
center does not maintain a permanent collection, but it is committed to presenting exhibitions and other programming developed in the spirit of experimentation embodied in the house.

Manhattan Beach Historical Society and Museum

1601 Manhattan Beach Boulevard, Manhattan Beach (Map No. 3)
310-374-7575
www.history90266.org

Open: Sa–Su, Noon–3:00 PM
Admission: Free
Parking: Street parking

In the early 1900s, Manhattan Beach served as a popular getaway for residents of Los Angeles and Pasadena. Traveling south via trolley or train, visitors would be met by realtors selling ocean-view property for prices unimaginable by today's standards. Development caught on and small cottages began to pop up all over town. One of these—a cozy 1905 building often referred to as the Little Red House for its rusty red-painted exterior—is where visitors will find this museum. Memorabilia, artifacts, everyday objects from the turn of the century, and an extensive photographs collection help illustrate the life and times of this small beach town, including its early growth, its popularity as a beach destination, and its residential, commercial, and social life. At the back of the house is a closet containing clothing from the early 1900s. Of note are several wool bathing suits that could be rented at the pier before spending a day at the sea. Interestingly, these one-piece outfits were for covering either men or women since it wasn't until 1933 that men could go topless on the beach.

Muller House Museum

1542 S. Beacon Street, San Pedro (Map No. 3)
310-831-1788

Open: Access to house by guided tour only, offered first three Sundays
of the month, 1:00–4:00 PM, or by appointment
Admission: Free
Parking: Street parking

This two-story Colonial Revival house was home to Captain
William A. Muller (1865–1936) and his family. Built in 1899 by
San Pedro founding citizen Edward Mahar, the house was purchased two years later by Muller, a prominent shipbuilder who
designed and constructed excursion vessels and some of the
first tug boats used in the harbor. The house has been moved
twice, the second time in 1984 when it was relocated to its current spot—a bluff overlooking the vast port and the San Pedro
Bay—and donated to the San Pedro Historical Society, an
organization dedicated to preserving the history of the harbor
and its impact on greater Los Angeles. Exhibiting items from
the historical society's growing collection, the museum is furnished to reflect life in the early 20th century in the active port
town. Muller's shipbuilding trade skills are evident in the
exquisitely crafted woodwork throughout the house, including
much of the wall paneling and doorways, the dining room
mantle, and ornate furniture.

Highlight:

A delicate antique dollhouse made in 1868

The Museum of African American Art

4005 Crenshaw Boulevard, 3rd Floor of Robinsons-May, Los Angeles
(Map No. 1)
323-294-7071
www.maaa-la.org
Open: Only during exhibitions—Th–Sa, 11:00 AM–6:00 PM; Su,
Noon–5:00 PM
Admission: Free; donations encouraged
Parking: Free in shopping mall lot

Shoppers and museumgoers unite in the Baldwin Hills
Crenshaw Plaza. Here, in a corner of the third floor of the
Robinsons-May department store is this museum, dedicated to
preserving and promoting art "by or about people of African
descent." The museum's unusual location, its founders say,
helps visitors embrace art as an accessible part of everyday life.
When temporary exhibitions are not on display, objects from
the museum's permanent collection are showcased. Chief
among its holdings are 40 paintings by Palmer C. Hayden
(1890–1973), a prominent artist of the Harlem Renaissance.

Highlight:
Palmer C. Hayden's John Henry series, honoring the legendary
railroad hero

The Museum of Contemporary Art, Grand Avenue*

250 S. Grand Avenue, Los Angeles (Map No. 1)

213-626-6222

www.moca.org

Open: M and F, 11:00 AM–5:00 PM; Th, 11:00 AM–8:00 PM; Sa–Su, 11:00 AM–6:00 PM

Admission: Adults, $8.00; Seniors and Students, $5.00; Children under 12, Free; also, free general admission on Thursdays, 5:00–8:00 PM

Parking: $8.00 with museum validation at Walt Disney Concert Hall garage (visit MOCA Web site for directions); also pay parking in other nearby lots and street parking

One institution in three venues, MOCA, as this museum is called for short, makes a lot of room for its esteemed permanent collection of American and European art created since 1940. At its main "branch" on downtown's Grand Avenue, built in red sandstone by architect Arata Isozaki, its more than 5,000 holdings in all visual media — painting, sculpture, drawings, prints, photographs, video, installations, and environmental works — show up in the galleries throughout the year. Grounding the collection are seminal works of Abstract Expressionist and Pop art, giving Angelenos and tourists the chance to take in works by Claes Oldenberg, Roy Lichtenstein, Mark Rothko, Franz Kline, and other heavy hitters in contemporary art. Painting, sculpture, photography, and drawings by Minimalist, Post-Minimalist, and Neo-Expressionist artists are well represented; more than 60 works by the likes of Dan Flavin and Cy Twombly, for example, have taken up residence here. Artists Sam Francis and Ed Moses have enriched MOCA's collections with major gifts of their work as well. The photography collection has been strengthened by the museum's mid-1990s acquisition of 2,300 documentary photographs by leading figures in the genre. Finally, the museum is committed to acquiring works by young and emerging artists as well as works by significant Southern California artists. Temporary exhibitions draw crowds to MOCA, too; recent shows have included such thematic presentations as *Ecstasy: In and About Altered States* and one-person retrospectives of featured artists Cindy Sherman and Robert Smithson.

Highlights:

Jackson Pollock's *Number 1, 1949* (1949)

Robert Rauschenberg's *Coca-Cola Plan* (1958)

Charles Ray's *Tabletop* (1989)

Liz Larner's *2 as 3 and Some, Too* (1997–1998)

Paul McCarthy's *Tokyo Santa, Santa's Trees* (1999)

*See separate entries about the museum's other two facilities, the Geffen Contemporary at MOCA and the Museum of Contemporary Art, Pacific Design Center.

The Museum of Contemporary Art, Pacific Design Center*

8687 Melrose Avenue, West Hollywood (Map No. 1)

213-626-6222

www.moca.org

Open: Tu–W and F, 11:00 AM–5:00 PM; Th, 11:00 AM–8:00 PM;
Sa–Su, 11:00 AM–6:00 PM

Admission: Free

Parking: 20 minutes free in Pacific Design Center lot, then $1.00 per 20 minutes thereafter, $10.00 maximum; also pay parking in nearby lots and street parking

Taking up 4,000 square feet of gallery space and a two-acre outdoor plaza, this facility of the Museum of Contemporary Art (MOCA) is in West Hollywood, in the can't-be-missed green-and-blue megabuilding designed by Cesar Pelli. Neighboring 150 showrooms of traditional and contemporary furnishings, this MOCA focuses on contemporary architecture and design, new work by established and emerging artists, and programs complementing the Grand Avenue venue's major exhibitions and permanent collection.

*See separate entries about the museum's other two facilities, the Museum of Contemporary Art, Grand Avenue, and the the Geffen Contemporary at MOCA.

Museum of Flying

www.museumofflying.com

Slated to reopen in 2007 in its new location, a large hangar at the Santa Monica Airport (exact address to be announced; check Web site for updates), this museum cares for a rare collection of World War II fighter aircraft. Most of these, according to museum officials, are in flight-ready condition. In the new facility, several of the awesome holdings will hang above visitors under a protective canopy extending from the side of the building. Back on the ground, exhibits will illustrate the glory days of the now-defunct Douglas Aircraft Company—most famous for its venerable DC series of commercial airplanes but also a leader in designing and building military aircraft—as well as other Southern California–based aviation and aerospace companies. An observation deck at the new site will give visitors a perfect vantage point from which to watch the active runway of the airport.

The Museum of Jurassic Technology

9341 Venice Boulevard, Culver City (Map No. 1)

310-836-6131

www.mjt.org

Open: Th, 2:00–8:00 PM; F–Su, Noon–6:00 PM

Recommended donation: Adults 22 and up, $5.00; "Unemployed persons," Persons 12–21, Seniors, and Students, $3.00; "Disabled persons" and "Active service personnel in uniform," $2.00; Children under 12, Free

Parking: Street parking

The brainchild of founder and curator David Wilson, this institution with the offbeat name is, as the orientation video explains, a throwback to when a museum was "a place for the Muses. . . where man's mind could attain a mood of aloofness above everyday affairs." And so, behind an unassuming store-front in Culver City, a labyrinth of rooms and hallways awaits visitors, enticing one and all to experience wonder for wonder's sake. Hundreds of rarities and curios abound, many assembled in elaborate dioramas, mood-enhanced by light and sound effects, and/or supported by deadpan audio commentary. One exhibit details the lifecycle of the Cameroonian stink ant, or *Megolaponera foetens*, whose tiny brain is overtaken by the spore of a fungus. Another sums up the ideas of a certain Geoffrey Sonnabend, the author of the reportedly revolutionary *Obliscence: Theories of Forgetting and the Problem of Matter*. Visitors are also invited to study precious artifacts gathered by mobile-home dwellers; the art of microminiaturist Hagop Sandaldjian, who handcrafted, between breaths and heartbeats in order to keep his hands still, impossibly tiny sculptures (of

Goofy and the Pope, for example) within the eyes of needles; and the horn that once protruded from the head of Mary Davis, whoever she may have been. Upstairs is the Borzoi Kabinet Theater, where visitors can catch a film about "a Cross-eyed Lefty from Tula and the Steel Flea." By the way, for those who may be wondering: indeed, this is the museum Lawrence Weschler investigated in his bestselling book *Mr. Wilson's Cabinet of Wonder*.

Additional highlights:

The gallery "No One May Ever Have the Same Knowledge Again: Letters to Mt. Wilson"

A live mouse on toast, a folk remedy for whooping cough

Museum of Latin American Art

628 Alamitos Avenue, Long Beach (Map No. 3)
562-437-1689
www.molaa.org

Open: Tu–Fr, 11:30 AM–7:00 PM; Sa, 11:00 AM–7:00 PM; Su, 11:00 AM–6:00 PM
Admission: Adults, $5.00; Seniors and Students, $3.00; Children under 12, Free; also, free general admission on Fridays

This museum is the only museum in the western United States to focus on contemporary Latin American fine art—that is, art created by artists who have lived and worked in Mexico, Central America, South America, and the Caribbean since World War II. The numerous paintings, drawings, prints, sculptures, and mixed-media works that comprise the museum's permanent holdings are rotated into temporary exhibitions throughout the year. Included here are works by internationally recognized artists; works by artists well-known in their native country but who enjoy little or no exposure in the United States; and lesser-known works by established artists, such as the sculpture *Sol Negro* by Fernando de Szyszlo. The museum exhibits art on long-term loan from the Smithsonian's Hirshhorn Museum and Sculpture Garden. The museum is currently undergoing an extensive expansion designed by Mexican architect Manuel Rosen.

Highlights:

Jorge Marín's bronze sculpture *Equilibrista en split* (2001)
Study for Soccer Players (1983) by Claudio Bravo

Museum of Neon Art

501 W. Olympic Boulevard, Suite 101, Los Angeles (Map No. 1)
213-489-9918
www.neonmona.org

Open: W–Sa, 11:00 AM–5:00 PM; Su, Noon–5:00 PM; second
Thursday of every month, 11:00 AM–8:00 PM
Admission: Adults, $5.00; Seniors and Students 13–22, $3.50;
Children under 13, Free; also, free general admission on second
Thursday of every month, 5:00–8:00 PM
Parking: Free parking during museum hours at Renaissance Tower
(Grand Avenue, south of 9th Street); also street parking

At this expectedly colorful, brightly lit museum, visitors have
the chance to view, at eye level, historic neon signage along
with contemporary works of electric and kinetic art. Founded
in 1981, the museum, or MONA, is the only one of its kind in
the world, and it literally blinks and buzzes with the sight and
sound of its holdings. In addition to its permanent collection of
works by more than 50 commercial and fine artists, MONA
also presents several changing exhibitions a year. A recent show
offered a retrospective of the great American beer sign. For an
informed, fun-filled look at the light and motion of today's
urban landscape, take one of MONA's popular nighttime bus
"cruises" to marvel at the neon signs, advertisements, and
movie marquees of Hollywood and downtown Los Angeles.

Highlights:

The first neon sign in the United States, illuminating the 1923
Packard logo created for a downtown Los Angeles car dealer

The sign of historic Hollywood hangout the Brown Derby,
memorable for its iconic hat and yellow lettering

The Museum of the San Fernando Valley

5800 Fulton Avenue, Valley Glen (Map No. 2)

818-947-2373

www.themuseumofthesanfernandovalley.org

Open: M, 1:00–3:00 PM; Tu, 5:00–7:00 PM; W, 10:00 AM–2:00 PM
Admission: Free
Parking: Street parking: also limited on-campus metered parking

Inside a modest bungalow on the campus of Los Angeles
Valley College is this museum, now in its 30th year. Here, students and visitors can consult books and view photographs,
maps, and objects pertaining to the San Fernando Valley. The
collection includes a handful of belongings of some of the
region's founding fathers, such as the stove of Colonel Isaac
Lankershim, who in 1869, along with fellow land developer
Isaac Newton Van Nuys, purchased a half-interest in the fertile
valley and would soon plant the seeds, literally, for its bountiful
agricultural industry. The museum also features a recreation of
the 1920s office of William Paul Whitsett, who established the
city of Van Nuys; memorabilia of several local women's clubs;
and a Dutch map dated 1715, which portrays California as an
island, a common cartographic error at the time.

Museum of Television & Radio

465 N. Beverly Drive, Beverly Hills (Map No. 1)

310-786-1025

www.mtr.org

Open: W–Su, Noon–5:00 PM

Recommended donation: Adults, $10.00; Seniors and Students, $8.00; Children under 14, $5.00

Parking: 2 hours free with museum validation in museum garage, $1.00 for each additional half hour; also pay parking in nearby lots and street parking

Want to relive the night when the Beatles thrilled millions on *The Ed Sullivan Show*? Or tune in to a few classic episodes of the radio drama *The Shadow*? Then spend an afternoon at the Museum of Television & Radio in Beverly Hills. Housing an identical collection to its older, sister museum in New York, the museum preserves the heritage of television and radio, giving the public access to more than 120,000 programs from the 1920s to the present. For up to two hours, visitors may watch or listen to programs of their choice at individual consoles — whether one's favorite episodes of *The Sopranos*, FDR's presidential radio addresses, MTV's first hour, Game Six of the 1977 World Series, or the premiere of *Sesame Street*. It's an added pleasure to get to hear or watch the commercials that aired during the shows. The museum also offers daily screenings and radio presentations in several theaters as well as specially-themed series and exhibitions. Architecture enthusiasts will note the museum building's design, by noted contemporary architect Richard Meier.

Museum of Tolerance

9786 W. Pico Boulevard, Los Angeles (Map No. 1)

310-553-8403

www.museumoftolerance.com

Open: M–Th, 11:00 AM–6:30 PM (last entry at 4:00 PM); F, 11:00 AM–3:00 PM (last entry at 1:00 PM); Su, 11:00 AM–7:30 PM (last entry at 5:00 PM)

Admission: For ToleranCenter and Holocaust Exhibit—Adults, $10.00; Seniors, $8.00; Students and Children under 12, $7.00; for special exhibition *Finding Our Families, Finding Ourselves*—Adults, $8.00; Seniors, $7.00; Students and Children under 12, $6.00; ask about discount rates when purchasing tickets to both the museum and *Finding Our Families, Finding Ourselves*; photo identification required for admission

Parking: Free in museum garage

At this experiential museum, an on-screen video host greets visitors with provocative questions about what it takes to live alongside peoples of diverse backgrounds. With these in mind, visitors make their way into the museum's ToleranCenter, which employs interactive video and Internet technology to engage one and all in exploring the meaning of tolerance, the consequences of hate, and the role of personal responsibility and choice in everyday life. Included here are the Millenium Machine, showing news report–like clips about international human rights abuses, and the Point of View Diner, dishing out divisive topics on video jukeboxes. The themes explored in the ToleranCenter give context to the theatrical galleries of the next section of the museum, the Holocaust Exhibit. Through video footage, dioramas, sound and light effects, narration, photographs, and maps, these galleries chronicle the rise and reign of Nazism, including a re-enactment of the Wannsee Conference, where Nazi leaders calculated "The Final Solution of the Jewish Question." On view in the museum's Multimedia Learning Center is its collection of artifacts and documents of the Holocaust, such as Nazi uniforms, objects made from desecrated Torah scroll parchments, and barbed wire from the concentration camps. *Finding Our Families, Finding Ourselves* is the museum's newest exhibit. It showcases the personal histories of noted Americans in diverse fields, from Maya Angelou to Joe Torre to Carlos Santana.

Highlights:

Ain't You Gotta Right, a 16-screen video wall screening extensive footage of the Civil Rights Movement in America

The Hall of Testimony, presenting first-hand accounts of the Holocaust and remembrances of its victims

Several original letters of Anne Frank

An American flag sewn by Mauthausen concentration camp inmates for their American liberators

Natural History Museum of Los Angeles County

900 Exposition Boulevard, Los Angeles (Map No. 1)
213-763-DINO (213-763-3466)
www.nhm.org

Open: M–F, 9:30 AM–5:00 PM; Sa–Su, 10:00 AM–5:00 PM.
Admission: Adults, $9.00; Seniors, Students, and Children 13–17,
$6.50; Children 5–12, $2.00; Children under 5, Free; also, free general admission on first Tuesday of every month; separate fee for the
Robinsons-May Pavilion of Wings
Parking: Pay parking in Exposition Park lots

A pair of towering dinosaur skeletons posed in battle greets
you in the Beaux Arts grand atrium of this, the largest museum
of natural history in the western United States. Seeking to foster understanding of and responsibility for the natural and cultural worlds, this long-revered cultural institution, the second
oldest in the city, holds more than 33 million eye-opening specimens and artifacts (only the Smithsonian Institution's National
Museum of Natural History holds more). Hundreds of
African and North American mammals, dinosaurs and
Cenozoic fossils, marine animals (including an awesome example of the megamouth, the world's rarest, most elusive shark, of
which only 17 have ever been found), birds, and other species
that have inhabited Earth throughout the ages are staged in
elaborate dioramas. Don't miss the museum's brilliant collection of gems and minerals. There is also a major gallery displaying ceramics, figurines, and other artifacts from prehistoric
Latin American societies, as well as a hall of California history
from the 1500s to the 1940s. Of unique interest is a gallery

exploring the rare ecosystem known as the chaparral, found in California and few places around the world, in which the plants and animals depend on fire for continued health and growth. Less than 1% of the museum's holdings are on view at any given time, so stop into the Director's Gallery for a changing display of selected treasures, personally chosen by the curators for highlight. The museum is kid-friendly throughout, but especially in the Discovery Center and the insect zoo where hands-on activities, like making fossil rubbings and feeding tarantulas, keep children busy. Also be sure to visit the museum's temporary exhibitions, which of late have been organized around ecological and environmental issues.

Additional highlights:

Every summer, the Robinsons-May Pavilion of Wings, featuring a landscaped environment of free-flying butterflies

The largest collection of gold in the U.S.

One of the world's finest *Tyrannosaurus rex* skulls on public view

The stunning rotunda

The Nethercutt Museum and San Sylmar

15151 and 15200 Bledsoe Street, Sylmar (Map No. 2)
818-364-6464 and 818-367-2251
www.nethercuttcollection.org

Open: Museum only—Tu–Sa, 9:00 AM–4:30 PM; access to San
Sylmar by advance reservation and guided tour only, Tu–Sa, 10:00 AM
and 1:30 PM; closed for two weeks around Christmas
Admission: Free
Parking: Free in museum lot

J.B. Nethercutt (1913–2004), co-founder of Merle Norman
Cosmetics, is the name behind this museum showcasing more
than 200 antique, classic, and specialty automobiles dating from
1898 to 1982. Every single car in the collection, the museum
proudly states, has been so well restored that it would drive like
new. The museum's new facility—built across the street from
the collection's original, marble-floored, and crystal-chande-
liered "salon" known as San Sylmar—provides 60,000 more
square feet in which to show off shiny examples of Packard,
Duesenberg, Pierce-Arrow, Rolls Royce, and other *crème de la
crème* makes. Included here are several Best-in-Show winners at
the Pebble Beach Concours d'Elegance. Throughout the
museum, emphasis is placed on important developments in
automotive design and engineering throughout history.
Unexpectedly, a group of mechanical musical instruments, such
as nickelodeons, Swiss bird boxes, and orchestians, is also part
of Nethercutt's collection. Organ recitals take place in the San
Sylmar building throughout the year; call ahead for schedule
and ticket information.

Highlights:

The 1912 Pullman railcar owned by the eldest daughter of California pioneer Lucky Baldwin

A Wurlitzer theater pipe organ

A 1967 Ferrari 365 California Spyder

A display of hood ornaments

Norton Simon Museum

411 W. Colorado Boulevard, Pasadena (Map No. 2)
626-449-6840
www.nortonsimon.org

Open: M, W–Th, and Sa–Su, Noon–6:00 PM; F, Noon–9:00 PM
Admission: Adults, $8.00; Seniors, $4.00; Students and Children under
18, Free; also, free general admission on first Friday of every month,
6:00–9:00 PM
Parking: Free in museum lot

European, Asian, and American art are on view in this museum, founded in 1924 as the Pasadena Art Institute and reorgan-
ized in 1974 by captain of industry and world-renowned art
collector Norton Simon (1907–1993). From the Renaissance to
the 20th century, with particular strength in Impressionist and
post-Impressionist art, the paintings, sculpture, and tapestries
assembled here are by such famed artists as Bellini, Botticelli,
Raphael, Rembrandt, Goya, van Gogh, Monet, Renoir, and
Manet. Also expect to see seminal works by Picasso, Matisse,
Klee, and Kandinsky. Rounding out the museum's holdings is
an important group of sculpture and artifacts from the Indian
subcontinent and Southeast Asia spanning two millennia. At
any given time, around 1,000 works from the collections fill the
galleries, which were redesigned in the late 1990s by Frank O.
Gehry working on the original building by Ladd & Kelsey. In
1999, the museum also unveiled a sculpture garden created by
landscape designer Nancy Goslee Power. Spend some time in
this setting inspired by Claude Monet's garden at Giverny and
showcasing the artistry of Henry Moore, Barbara Hepworth,
and many more. Also displayed outdoors, on a lower level, are

several works from the Asian sculpture collection bathing in natural light and surrounded by greenery.

Highlights:

Galka Scheyer's "Blue Four" Collection of Kandinsky, Klee, Jawlensky, and Feininger works

Nagapattinam-stone seated Buddha

Vincent van Gogh's *Portrait of a Peasant* (1888)

The Degas Collection, with more than 100 paintings, prints, pastels, and sculpture, including the artist's model bronzes

Francisco de Zurbarán's *Still Life with Lemons, Oranges, and a Rose* (1633)

The Oran Z Pan African Black Facts and Wax Museum

3742 W. Martin Luther King, Jr. Boulevard, Los Angeles (Map No. 1)
323-299-8829
www.oransblackmuseum.com

Open: Tu, 11:00 AM–4:00 PM, or by appointment
Admission: Free
Parking: Free in adjacent lot

Founded by local businessman and passionate collector Oran Z. Belgrave, this museum pays respect to African and African American history, art, and culture. Filling its rooms is a vast accumulation of photographs, postcards, sheet music, coins, books, toys, kitchenware, and much more. Visitors will see such items as ancient Egyptian artifacts, slave records, Civil Rights Movement–era memorabilia, and artful textiles, including handwoven quilts from Zimbabwe that tell stories in pictures square by square and centuries-old silk Kente cloths from Ghana. This wide-ranging collection is continually being augmented by Belgrave's latest acquisitions from his travels around the world. Special exhibits stress the integral role that African Americans—as inventors, politicians, civic leaders, entertainers, and sports figures—have played in the life of our nation. Also on view are a number of wax figures of illustrious African Americans, including Malcolm X, Ralph Bunche, Dorothy Dandridge, Jackie Robinson, and Billie Holiday.

Highlights:

A 1952 50-cent piece with the faces of Booker T. Washington and George Washington Carver on the front

A well-worn, autographed Joe Lewis boxing glove

Pacific Asia Museum

46 N. Los Robles Avenue, Pasadena (Map No. 4)
626-449-2742
www.pacificasiamuseum.org

Open: W–Th and Sa–Su, 10:00 AM–5:00 PM; F, 10:00 AM–8:00 PM
Admission: Adults, $7.00; Seniors and Students, $5.00; also, free
general admission on fourth Friday of every month
Parking: Free in museum lot; also street parking

Occupying a distinctly Chinese Imperial Palace–style ornamented building with an upturned tiled roof is this museum
specializing in the art of Asia and the Pacific Islands. Its more
than 15,000 representative examples of art and artifacts from
these regions span more than 5,000 years. Opening galleries
display the museum's extensive collection of Chinese ceramics
ranging from the simplest handbuilt earthenware to the finest
Imperial porcelains. Proceed into subsequent galleries to see
museum holdings of Southeast Asian and Indian sculpture,
artifacts and ritual objects from Papua New Guinea and West
Papua, Himalayan and South Asian Buddhist art, Japanese and
Chinese decorative arts, Cambodian and Thai ceramics, as well
as paintings, woodblock prints, and calligraphy. Changing exhibitions are also presented at the museum. Between galleries,
step outside into the courtyard to see the koi pond and two
marble Chinese lions standing guard.

Highlights:

A hands-on ceramic study gallery where visitors can learn
more about how ceramics are made and decorated

Chinese jade objects dating back to the Neolithic-period Qing
dynasty

Page Museum at the La Brea Tar Pits

5801 Wilshire Boulevard, Los Angeles (Map No. 1)
323-934-PAGE (323-934-7243)
www.tarpits.org

Open: M–F, 9:30 AM–5:00 PM; Sa–Su, 10:00 AM–5:00 PM
Admission: Adults, $7.00; Seniors and Students, $4.50; Children
5–12, $2.00; Children under 5, Free; also, free general admission on
first Tuesday of every month
Parking: Pay parking in museum lot, discounted with validation; also
street parking

It's hard to imagine but 10,000 to 40,000 years ago, during the
late Pleistocene Epoch, or Ice Age, the land that is now Los
Angeles was roamed by saber-toothed cats, dire wolves, mammoths, mastodons, ancient camels, and giant ground sloths.
Thousands of these now-extinct creatures met a cruel fate
when they stepped foot into any of a number of oozing, bub-
bling asphalt pools now known as the La Brea Tar Pits.
Unable to escape the sticky tar, the beasts perished in this
death trap, leaving behind a bounty of well-preserved remains,
which comprises this museum's extraordinary collection of fossils, nearly three million in number. Come see reconstructed
skeletons and robotic sculptures of these prehistoric specimens
and take a look at some of the tar pits themselves. In addition,
watch paleontologists at work inside a functioning laboratory
located behind windows in the galleries. Finally, take a minute
to read up on the museum's founder and namesake, George C.
Page, who was responsible for making the fruit basket wrapped
in cellophane the popular gift item it is today.

Highlights:

More than 30 complete skeletons of fossil mammals and birds

Wall display of 404 dire wolf skulls

A 40,000-year-old wood fragment, the museum's oldest fossil

Pasadena Museum of California Art

490 E. Union Street, Pasadena (Map No. 4)
626-568-3665
www.pmcaonline.org

Open: W–Su, Noon–5:00 PM
Admission: Adults, $6.00; Seniors and Students, $4.00; Children under
12, Free; also, free general admission on first Friday of every month
Parking: Free in museum garage; also street parking

This young institution is devoted to California art, architecture,
and design from 1850, the year California achieved statehood,
to the present. Its incipient permanent collection will soon be
augmented by the 20th-century California paintings acquired
over the years by the museum's founders, Pasadena art collec-
tors Robert and Arlene Oltman. In the meantime, since opening in 2002, the museum has focused exclusively on temporary
exhibitions of both historic and evolving work made in
California in a variety of media and styles. Artists whose creations have been exhibited here include Alson Clark, Gary
Baseman, Raimonds Staprans, and Frederick Hammersley.
The museum's three-story building was designed by Los
Angeles architects Steve Johnson and Jim Favaro, who have
gifted visitors with a public roof terrace overlooking Old
Pasadena with the San Gabriel Mountains in the distance.
Interestingly, the Oltmans' private residence is also situated up
there, atop the very museum they established.

Highlights:

The garage, enlivened by the work of renowned graffiti artist
Kenny Scharf

Pasadena Museum of History

470 W. Walnut Street, Pasadena (Map No. 2)
626-577-1660
www.pasadenahistory.org

Open: History Center—W–Su, Noon–5:00 PM; access to Fenyes
Mansion and Finnish Folk Art Museum by guided tour only, W–Su, 1:30
and 3:00 PM; research library, preferably by appointment, Sa–Su,
1:00–4:00 PM
Admission: For History Center—Adults, $5.00, Children under 12,
Free; for tour of Fenyes Mansion and Finnish Folk Art Museum—
Adults, $4.00; Children under 12, Free; ask about senior and student
discounts
Parking: Free in museum lot

To learn about the city of Pasadena and its neighboring communities, come to this museum, founded in 1924 to preserve
documents and artifacts relating to the western San Gabriel
Valley. More than one million historic photographs, rare
books, manuscripts, maps, architectural records, costumes, and
paintings spanning 1797 to the present are maintained in the
archives. They may also be found in the History Center galleries as part of the museum's many changing exhibitions about
Pasadena's heritage.

Visitors should also tour the 13-room Fenyes Mansion and its
two acres of landscaped grounds, which were donated to and
became the headquarters of the museum in 1970. Now listed
on the National Register of Historic Places, the elegant 1906
Beaux Arts residence was designed by Robert D. Farquhar
(with a later addition by Sylvanus Marston) for the eminent

Fenyes family. Except for a few rooms on the upper floors, this architectural jewel contains its original antiques, family heirlooms, and various personal items (even the medicines and spices in the cabinets belonged to the Fenyeses), giving visitors a taste of how the Pasadena elite lived and luxuriated in the early 20th century. Also left behind is the family's art collection, with paintings by William Merritt Chase, Benjamin C. Brown, Richard E. Miller, and other leading American artists of their day.

Starting in 1947, owing to the marriage of the Fenyes granddaughter to the first Finnish Consul to Southern California, Y.A. Paloheimo, the Fenyes Mansion served as the Finnish Consulate for 17 years. In 1949, Paloheimo transplanted onto the grounds a Swiss chalet–style redwood garage from a nearby estate and turned it into a guesthouse and traditional Finnish sauna. Designed by Frederick Roehrig, it now serves as the Finnish Folk Art Museum, operated by the Pasadena Museum of History in partnership with the Finlandia Foundation. Here visitors will find furniture typically found in a traditional 19th-century Finnish *tupa*, or farmhouse, along with Finnish folk art spanning many centuries and hailing from across Finland. This is the only display of its kind outside of Finland.

Highlights:
Pasadena Tournament of Roses Collection of programs
The *Pasadena Star-News* Historic Archives
Antique 16th-century walnut cabinet from Spain
Artwork by family matriarch and *plein air* painter Eva Fenyes

The Paul Gray PC Museum

130 E. Ninth Street, Claremont (Map No. 4)
909-621-8209
www.cgu.edu/pages/2057.asp
Open: M–F, 8:00 AM–10:00 PM; Sa–Su, 10:00 AM–5:00 PM
Admission: Free
Parking: Street parking

Several display cases in the corridors of the School of
Information Systems and Technology at Claremont Graduate
University comprise this museum of the personal computer
(PC). The many desktops, laptops, printers, user manuals,
mouses, and monitors help to mark the leaps-and-bounds
advances in PC technology over the years. Check out the 1983
GRID Compass, the first "clamshell"-designed, battery-pow-
ered laptop, which would set the standard for today's laptops.
It originally sold for no less than $8,000! Also view a model of
the first portable PC, the Osborne I, which premiered at the
West Coast Computer Faire in 1981 weighing in at a hefty 23
1/2 pounds.

Petersen Automotive Museum

6060 Wilshire Boulevard, Los Angeles (Map No. 1)
323-930-CARS (323-930-2277)
www.petersen.org

Open: Main galleries—Tu–Su and most holiday Mondays, 10:00
AM–6:00 PM; May Family Discovery Center—Tu–F, 10:00 AM–4:00
PM and Sa–Su, 10:00 AM–5:00 PM
Admission: Adults, $10.00; Seniors, Students, and Active Military
$5.00; Children 5–12, $3.00; Children under 5, Free
Parking: Pay parking in museum lot; also street parking

Welcoming one and all to prize "one of humankind's greatest achievements," this museum explores a century of the automobile and its impact on American culture, especially in Southern California. Dozens of rare and classic cars, trucks, and motorcycles are displayed in more than 30 lifelike dioramas—a turn-of-the-century blacksmith shop, a 1920s gas station, and a mid-century suburban tract house, to name a few—each designed to illustrate a chapter in automotive history. Visitors learn how the automobile gave rise to drive-in businesses, custom body work, garages, highway patrol, billboards, auto malls, AAA, pumping stations, alleys (built to keep traffic flowing on the main thoroughfares), and other lasting features of everyday life. The museum also uses five showroom-like galleries to mount changing exhibitions and to flaunt race cars, hot rods, celebrity cars, and much more from its collection. A hands-on children's "discovery center" teaches future drivers the basic science behind automotive technology.

Highlights:

1939 Bugatti, Type 57-C by Vanvooren, originally owned by the Prince of Persia Mohammed Reza Pahlavi

1947 Cisitalia, 202 Coupe by Pinin Farina

The Hotwheels® Hall of Fame

The futuristic taxi from *Blade Runner*

Petterson Museum of Intercultural Art

730 Plymouth Road, Claremont (Map No. 4)
909-399-5544
www.pilgrimplace.org/asp/Site/OurServices/PettersonMuseum/view.asp
Open: F–Su, 2:00–4:00 PM
Admission: Free
Parking: Free in facility lot

Situated on the grounds of Pilgrim Place, a community for retired church professionals, this museum seeks to promote an appreciation of world cultures through its rich, growing collection of international arts and crafts, brought to Pilgrim Place by retiring missionaries, pastors, and other donors. Rotated into exhibitions throughout the year, the museum's holdings include statues, stained glass, paintings, porcelain figurines and vases, textiles, costumes, masks, ceramics, and more. Recent exhibitions have included *Celebrating the Arts of the Caribbean Islands*, featuring cloth dolls, steel drums and other musical instruments, and wood carvings from the region, as well as *Mola Art of the Kuna Indians from the San Blas Islands*. Visitors may also wish to peruse art books from around the world in the museum's library, open during regular museum hours.

Highlights:

A large, ornate Japanese cloisonné vase from the 1870s

A carved wooden cabinet from China from the late 1800s or early 1900s

Plaza Fire House Museum

125 Paseo de la Plaza, Los Angeles (Map No. 1)
213-680-2525
www.cityofla.org/ELP/fire.htm

Open: Tu–Su, 10:00 AM–3:00 PM
Admission: Free
Parking: Pay parking in nearby lots; also street parking

Erected in 1884, the Plaza Fire House was the first building constructed by the City of Los Angeles to house firefighting equipment and personnel. Designed by architect William Boring, it was modeled after a popular station design in his native Illinois, with horses stabled inside the station as was the custom in colder climates. Today it is a museum that preserves firefighting history and memorabilia. On display are tools and equipment from the late 19th and early 20th centuries, such as helmets, extinguishers, and pumps, as well as vintage photographs and maps. The State Division of Architecture ensured that all of the distinct features of Boring's original design were reconstructed, such as the turntable in the floor. This contraption allowed for a horse-drawn fire carriage to be spun around as necessary so that its horses would never have to back in or out of the building. The Plaza Fire House is part of El Pueblo de Los Angeles Historical Monument, which marks the city's birthplace.

Pomona College Museum of Art

333 N. College Way, Claremont (Map No. 4)
909-621-8283
www.pomona.edu/museum

Open: Tu–F, Noon–5:00 PM; Sa–Su, 1:00–5:00 PM
Admission: Free
Parking: Street parking

This university museum presents temporary shows throughout the year in addition to its ongoing Project Series, which introduces new forms, techniques, or concepts being explored by experimental Southern California artists. The museum also cares for the college's diverse collections of fine art. Among its key holdings are 13 works of European art, predominantly Christian in subject matter and including a number of luminous Italian panel paintings by 15th-century artists like Neri di Bicci. These were donated to the college in 1961 by five-and-dime-store entrepreneur and philanthropist Samuel H. Kress. The museum is also known for its more than 5,000 Native American artifacts. These holdings are strong in California and Southwestern basketry, Southwestern ceramics, and beadwork of the Plains and Great Lakes. The museum's collection of prints, drawings, and photographs is also growing, owing to several important gifts and purchases. These acquisitions have brought in works by masters of photography D.O. Hill and Robert Adamson, Robert Capa, Aaron Siskind, and more. While on campus, wander over to Frary Hall to look upon two murals maintained by the museum: *Prometheus* by Mexican artist José Clemente Orozco and *Genesis* by Italian-born American painter Rico Lebrun.

Additional highlights:

An English alabaster relief (c. 1400–1425) portraying the Virgin Mary flanked by not one but both her parents, a rarely-seen composition

First-edition sets of all of printmaker and social satirist Francisco de Goya's etching series

Ramona Museum of California History

339 S. Mission Avenue, San Gabriel (Map No. 4)

626-288-2026

www.ramonamuseum.org

Open: Sa, 1:00–4:00 PM

Admission: Free

Parking: Free in museum lot

More than 125 years since its founding as a fraternal group cultivating mutual support, intellectual engagement, and friendship among its members, the Native Sons of the Golden West has evolved into a body of spirited Californians dedicated to the history of their state, from its Native American roots to statehood. The so-called Ramona Parlor #109 is the second largest of many parlors that comprise the Native Sons and the only one that, among its many vocations, owns and operates a museum. Here one can view a potpourri of objects gathered by Ramona members since before the turn of the century, such as a cribbage board carved by a San Quentin inmate, artifacts from the earthquake that rocked San Francisco in 1906, and the opera glasses of Pio Pico, the last Mexican governor of California.

Raymond M. Alf Museum of Paleontology

1175 W. Baseline Road, Claremont (Map No. 4)
909-624-2798
www.alfmuseum.org

Open: All year round, M–F, 8:00 AM–Noon and 1:00–4:00 PM; during
school year (September–May), Sa, Noon–3:00 PM; closed during win-
ter and spring breaks (check Web site for exact dates)
Admission: Adults and Children 5 and up, $3.00; Children under 5,
Free
Parking: Free in facility lot

There's a lot to dig into at the Webb Schools in Claremont.
The institution's paleontology museum, the only museum on a
high school campus accredited by the American Association of
Museums, has collected more than 70,000 specimens.
Practically all have been excavated by Webb faculty, students,
and alumni. The museum got its start in the early 1930s when
biology teacher Raymond M. Alf began organizing field trips
in search of fossils. In 1936, he and a group of students came
upon the skull of a new species of peccary, or fossil pig, a find
that would prompt the official founding of the museum. In the
decades since, the collection has grown in volume and prestige.
The museum's Hall of Life takes visitors on a journey through
the history of life. Here are displayed, among other treasures,
dinosaur eggs from China and Mongolia and just some of the
museum's 14,000 fossil invertebrates. The Hall of Footprints
presents a collection of fossilized footprints, recognized as one
of the largest and most diverse in the world. The creatures
whose steps can be tracked here include ancient camels, spiders,
reptiles, and dinosaurs.

Highlights:

A trackway of the giant bear-dog known as *Amphicyon*

Fossil teeth from extinct primates and marsupials unearthed in California

A massive alligator skull from the Amazon

Redondo Beach Historical Museum

302 Flagler Lane, Redondo Beach (Map No. 3)
310-372-0197
www.redondobeachhistorical.org

Open: W, 10:00 AM–1:00 PM; Sa–Su, Noon–4:00 PM
Admission: Free
Parking: Free parking in Heritage Court's lot

Redondo Beach's Heritage Court came to be when preservationists needed a place to relocate up to three turn-of-the-century historic houses. Two structures have already been moved, and it is inside one of them, a circa 1890s Queen Anne–style cottage, where the Redondo Beach Historical Society presents its collection of memorabilia relating to the city. An early port of Los Angeles, Redondo Beach served a thriving shipping industry in the late 19th and early 20th centuries. It was also where beach lovers from Los Angeles and Pasadena often spent the day or the weekend. Among many exhibits, one photographic montage illustrates the city's schools, businesses, pier, recreational pastimes, and famous residents over the years. Another display remembers George Freeth, the legendary surfer, swimmer, and diver who came to Redondo Beach in the early 1900s from Hawaii and eventually became Southern California's first official lifeguard.

Highlight:

A photograph of Redondo Plunge, built in 1908 as the first salt water indoor swimming tank with a capacity for 2,000 bathers

Ripley's Believe It or Not! Odditorium

6780 Hollywood Boulevard, Los Angeles (Map No. 1)

323-466-6335

www.ripleys.com/hollywood.html

Open: Mid-June to Labor Day, Su–Th, 9:00 AM–11:00 PM and F–Sa, 9:00 AM–midnight; rest of year, Su–Th, 10:00 AM–10:30 PM and F–Sa, 10:00 AM–11:30 PM

Admission: Adults, $11.95; Children 5–12, $7.95; Children under 5, Free

Parking: Pay parking in nearby lots; also street parking

Like the former *Ripley's Believe It or Not!* comic strip and television shows, this museum on Hollywood Boulevard lays claim to "where truth is stranger than fiction." Here's where superlatives of size, quantity, rarity, and incredibility are celebrated. The man behind the famed brand name is Robert Ripley, a world traveler whose quest to acquire what he considered bizarre from every corner of the globe gave rise to one of the world's largest chains of attractions. In the Hollywood facility—with an enormous dinosaur statue exploding out of the roof, it's not hard to find—one can check out more than 300 curiosities meant to astonish and amaze, many of them collected or documented by Ripley himself. Dioramas and video clips stand in for the unbelievable people, places, things, feats, and abilities that can't be shown in the original.

Highlights:

A portrait of John Wayne made of laundry lint

Toothpick Golden Gate Bridge, a sculpture built from 30,000 toothpicks

Genuine skeleton of a two-headed baby

Ruth and Charles Gilb Arcadia Historical Museum

380 W. Huntington Drive, Arcadia (Map No. 4)

626-574-5440

www.ci.arcadia.ca.us/home/index.asp?page=815

Open: Tu–Sa, 10:00 AM–4:00 PM

Admission: Free

Parking: Free in museum lot

The San Gabriel Valley city of Arcadia and surrounding areas were once the Native American village known as Aleupkigna, or "land of many waters." The Tongva tribe who lived here benefited from the moisture-rich lands of the valley, as did the Spanish, who founded the San Gabriel Mission nearby along with Rancho Santa Anita, a vast agricultural outpost encompassing present-day Arcadia. Following Mexican rule first, then American statehood, Elias J. "Lucky" Baldwin purchased, in 1875, about 8,000 acres, selling some but keeping for himself an impressive homestead and ranch. An ambitious man, he was as responsible for the orange groves, irrigation systems, and other measures as he was for the gambling halls, saloons, and the Santa Anita Race Track. In 1903, Baldwin took a portion of his property and established the city of Arcadia, with himself as first mayor. More than 100 years later, the museum, named for its lead donors, seeks to preserve this history. On display in the museum is the Arcadia Historical Society's collection of artifacts, period furnishings, photographs, and memorabilia.

San Fernando Museum of Art and History

519 S. Brand Boulevard, San Fernando (Map No. 2)
818-838-6360
Open: W–Su, 11:00 AM–3:00 PM
Admission: Free
Parking: Street parking

This young museum opened its doors in 2005 with a mission to promote the cultural and fine arts of historic San Fernando. As the museum's permanent collection begins to grow, visitors can expect to view art, artifacts, documents, and photographs on loan from local residents and historical societies. Many of these tell the story of the various immigrant groups that have settled in the area at different times, including the Spanish and the Japanese, as well as the Italians, who made a living growing olive groves as they did back in Italy. Visitors will also learn about key figures in San Fernando history, including Charles Maclay, who purchased a significant portion of the north San Fernando Valley in 1874 and founded the town of San Fernando.

San Gabriel Mission Museum

427 S. Junipero Serra Drive, San Gabriel (Map No. 4)

626-457-3048

www.sangabrielmission.org

Open: Daily, 9:00 AM–4:30 PM

Admission: Adults, $5.00; Seniors, $4.00; Children 6–17, $3.00; Children under 6, Free

Parking: Free in facility lot

The San Gabriel Mission Arcángel, the fourth of 21 California missions founded, was established on September 8, 1771, and mass has been said here every day since. Built from 1791 to 1805 and restored following the 1987 Whittier earthquake, the mission church retains many of its original features, including the main altar, which was transported from Mexico City in the 1790s, and the 300-year-old painting *Our Lady of Sorrows*. Legend has it that when the Indians who were occupying the San Gabriel Valley were shown the painting by the missionaries, they were so moved by its beauty that they abandoned plans to drive the Europeans away and offered friendship and service instead. Among many other points of interest, a walk on the grounds will take visitors past the oldest graveyard in Los Angeles County, as well as vats for making soap and candles, since the San Gabriel Mission once supplied both commodities to most of the other missions. In a tile-roofed adobe brick building next to the old winery is the museum. Displayed here are priests' vestments dating back to the 18th century, a Spanish bedroom set from 1623, and an array of tools, books, crosses, devotional statues and paintings, musical instruments, and furniture used by the mission over the centuries.

Highlights:

A handpainted red silk priest's vestment made in China and presented to the mission in 1783

The so-called Aboriginal Paintings of the 14 Stations of the Cross

A lavishly illustrated, sheepskin-bound Bible, printed in 1588 in Venice, Italy

Santa Monica Historical Society Museum

1539 Euclid Street, Santa Monica* (Map No. 1)
310-395-2290
www.santamonicahistory.org

Open: Tu–F, 10:00 AM–4:30 PM; second and fourth Sundays of every month, 1:00–4:00 PM
Admission: Adults, $5.00; Seniors and Students, $2.00; Children under 12, Free
Parking: Limited free parking in museum lot; also street parking

In 1975, upon the centennial of the city of Santa Monica, residents of the bayside community approved the founding of the Santa Monica Historical Society. It was to serve as caretaker of the city's history and promoter of local art and culture. In 1988, the organization opened a museum for the collection and display of objects and memorabilia relating to Santa Monica. Included are historic documents, maps, telephone directories, rare books, school yearbooks, textiles, paintings, artifacts, and more than 500,000 photographs that illustrate the story of Santa Monica and give residents a sense of belonging and civic pride. Here is where to learn how local landmarks such as the Third Street Promenade and the Santa Monica Pier came to be. A permanent photographic exhibition, *Cities by the Sea*, offers a pictorial history of Santa Monica and the surrounding neighborhoods of Ocean Park, Pacific Palisades, Malibu, Venice, and the Santa Monica Canyon.

*The museum is scheduled to change locations in late 2006. Check Web site for updates on this relocation.

Santa Monica Museum of Art

Bergamot Station G1, 2525 Michigan Avenue, Santa Monica
(Map No. 1)
310-568-6488
www.smmoa.org

Open: Tu–Sa, 11:00 AM–6:00 PM
Recommended donation: Adults, $5.00; Seniors and Students, $3.00
Parking: Free in museum lot; also street parking

This museum does not have a permanent collection but mounts temporary exhibitions of "the art of our time," often by whom it considers underknown artists. One recent show celebrated the creativity and influence of the enigmatic West Coast Beat artist Wallace Berman, while another was the first major museum retrospective of the work of Ant Farm, the underground architecture, video, performance, and installation collective. The museum is located in the complex of art galleries known as Bergamot Station, so make an afternoon of it and stroll around to take in even more art.

Skirball Cultural Center

2701 N. Sepulveda Boulevard, Los Angeles (Map No. 1)

310-440-4500

www.skirball.org

Open: Tu–W and F–Sa, Noon–5:00 PM; Th, Noon–9:00 PM; Su, 11:30 AM–5:00 PM

Admission: Adults, $8.00; Seniors and Students, $6.00; Children under 12, Free; also, free general admission on Thursdays

Parking: Free in facility lots

Nestled in the hills connecting West Los Angeles and the San Fernando Valley, this cultural center houses, in its museum, one of the premiere Judaica collections in the Western hemisphere. More than 30,000 objects—including archaeological artifacts, ceremonial objects from around the world, items drawn from everyday American Jewish life, and thousands of graphics, paintings, sculptures, and fine art in a variety of other media—are gathered here to portray some 4,000 years of Jewish history. These holdings reveal much about the daily life, beliefs, customs, worship, and artistic production of Jews throughout the Diaspora from biblical to contemporary times. Throughout the museum's core exhibition, *Visions and Values: Jewish Life from Antiquity to America*, emphasis is placed on how the story of the Jewish people coming to realize their hopes in the United States—with its myriad struggles and opportunities—in many ways mirrors the experiences of diverse immigrant groups. In addition to changing exhibitions, the Skirball as a cultural center is also committed to presenting theater, dance, music, film, and literary programs, as well as children's activities and continuing education classes. While visiting the

Skirball, take time to wander its 15-acre grounds, designed by architect Moshe Safdie. In 2007, the Skirball will open a new, major family-oriented gallery, based on the Noah's Ark story. This destination will meaningfully explore the themes of diversity, community, and new beginnings.

Highlights:

Statue of Liberty Hanukkah lamp by Manfred Anson (1986)

Illuminated Jewish marriage contracts from Italy from the 18th century

Bronze bust of Abraham Lincoln by Sir Moses Ezekiel

The original typescript Nuremberg Laws, bearing Adolf Hitler's signature, on indefinite loan from the Huntington Library

South Pasadena Historical Museum

913 Meridian Street, South Pasadena (Map No. 1)
626-799-9089
www.sppreservation.org

Open: Th, 3:00–8:00 PM; Sa, 1:00–4:00 PM
Admission: Free
Parking: Free in facility lot; also street parking

Known for its old-fashioned, small-town ambience, South Pasadena became a prime residential suburb of Los Angeles with the completion of the Pacific Electric Short Line in 1903. The South Pasadena Preservation Foundation aims to foster appreciation of this and other milestones in the city's heritage. It started this museum in 1987 to exhibit photographs, artifacts, and memorabilia tracing the history of the area, including nostalgic looks at local landmarks of yesteryear, such as the Raymond Hotel and the Cawston Ostrich Farm. The museum is housed inside one of the foundation's restoration projects, the 1887 Meridian Iron Works, a quaint building with a late-Victorian storefront façade, which first served as a hotel and a general store and later became a busy blacksmith shop.

The S.S. *Lane Victory* Museum

Berth 94, San Pedro (Map No. 3)
310-519-9545
www.lanevictory.org
Open: Daily, 9:00 AM–4:00 PM
Admission: Adults, $3.00; Children under 16, $1.00
Parking: Free for one hour in facility lots

Anchored in a slip in the Port of Los Angeles, the S.S. *Lane Victory* endures as a living memorial to the civil merchant marine. Built in 1944, the ship served in the final days of World War II as well as in the Korean and Vietnam Wars. In 1989, it returned to the Los Angeles Harbor, where it was built, to be fully restored. Today, visitors of all ages can board the 10,750-ton, fully-operational cargo ship to experience the inner workings of this historic vessel. On deck, visitors can "man" the wartime armament located along the rim of the ship, while below deck they can explore its cargo holds and seamen's quarters. The ship is a floating museum in and of itself, but there is in fact a dedicated gallery within its hatches of World War II artifacts and ship memorabilia, such as nautical equipment, uniforms, medals, newspaper clippings from 1940 to 1946, and an extensive assortment of meticulously built merchant marine models. Another "museum" hatch in the ship contains a 20-ton triple-expansion steam engine — similar to what powered the *Titanic* — as well as several Jeeps used during World War II. Guided tours of the captain's bridge and the not-to-be-missed engine room, where visitors can fathom the immense, complex power needed to operate the S.S. *Lane Victory*, are available by advance appointment.

Torrance Art Museum

3320 Civic Center Drive, Torrance (Map No. 3)
310-618-6340
www.torranceartmuseum.com

Open: Tu–Sa, Noon–6:00 PM
Admission: Free
Parking: Free in Civic Center lots

This cultural destination in Los Angeles's South Bay area presents temporary exhibitions of contemporary art organized around provocative themes. One recent show of various artists' works, *Telling*, probed issues surrounding the divulgence of information; another show took a look at the flourish as an invocation of visual pleasure. The museum also brings together artwork by members of community arts organizations and by students of local school districts. The museum recently underwent a significant expansion, so visitors can expect even more exhibitions here throughout the year.

Torrance Historical Society and Museum

1345 Post Avenue, Torrance (Map No. 3)
310-328-5392
www.visittorrance.com/historical.htm
Open: Tu–Th and Su, 1:00–4:00 PM
Admission: Free
Parking: Street parking

Located in the city's former main public library, this museum aims to preserve the history of Torrance and Rancho San Pedro, the Spanish land grant given to soldier Juan Jose Dominguez in 1784 of which Torrance was a part. At the turn of the 20th century, Pasadena businessman Jared Sidney Torrance purchased 3,500 acres of land from Dominguez's heirs with the intention of developing the area into a model city—a totally planned community halfway between Los Angeles and the San Pedro Harbor that would achieve a balanced mix of residential, commercial, and industrial space. The museum's collection of photographs, books, maps, newspaper clippings, memorabilia, and artifacts traces this development and other key moments in the city's history. Among these is when Torrance was awarded the All-America City honor by the National League of Cities, an accomplishment documented in the congratulatory telegram from President Dwight Eisenhower to the mayor.

Additional highlights:
Artist's mural depicting the history of the city of Torrance
Silver-plated trophy awarded to Torrance on New Year's Day 1914 for its entry into the Rose Parade

Travel Town Transportation Museum

5200 Zoo Drive, Griffith Park, Los Angeles (Map No. 2)
323-662-5874
www.cityofla.org/RAP/grifmet/tt/

Open: M–F, 10:00 AM–4:00 PM; Sa–Su, 10:00 AM–5:00 PM
Admission: Museum only—free; separate fee for miniature train ride—
Adults and Children, $2.00; Seniors, $1.50
Parking: Free in museum lot

Train lovers, head to this family destination and outdoor museum located in Los Angeles's Griffith Park. Designed by its founders to serve as a "railroad petting zoo," Travel Town encourages one and all to climb onto its antique locomotives, freight cars, passenger cars, and cabooses. Together these trace the history of railroad transportation in the western United States from the 1880s through the 1930s, with emphasis on how the railways fueled the development of Southern California. Be sure to take the kids aboard Travel Town's miniature train ride, which choo-choos along the perimeter of the museum grounds.

Highlight:

The well-preserved locomotive and visitor favorite *Mariposa*, built in 1864 by Lancaster Locomotive Works

UCLA Armand Hammer Museum of Art and Cultural Center

10899 Wilshire Boulevard, Los Angeles (Map No. 1)

310-443-7000

www.hammer.ucla.edu

Open: Tu–W and F–Sa, 11:00 AM–7:00 PM; Th, 11:00 AM–9:00 PM;
Su, 11:00 AM–5:00 PM; Grunwald Center by appointment only
Admission: Adults, $5.00; Seniors and UCLA alumni, $3.00; Students
and Children under 18 with an adult, Free; also, free general admission on Thursdays
Parking: Pay parking in museum garage; also, pay parking in nearby
lots and street parking

This museum, now operated by the University of California, Los Angeles, was founded by the late Dr. Armand Hammer, art collector, philanthropist, and former chairman of Occidental Petroleum Corporation. Situated next door to Occidental's international headquarters, "The Hammer" exhibits contemporary and historical work in all media. While temporary exhibitions (often of cutting-edge art) open here year round, selections from the museum's four permanent collections are always on view as well. The Armand Hammer Collection consists primarily of 19th-century French art, with works by Claude Monet, Camille Pisarro, Jean-Baptiste-Camille Corot, among many others. Four paintings by Vincent van Gogh also belong to this collection, as do a small group of European Old Master paintings and numerous works by 18th- to 20th-century American artists such as Mary Cassatt and Andrew Wyeth. The museum is home to one of the world's most extensive holdings of the prints, drawings, paintings, and sculpture of 19th-century French caricaturist Honoré Daumier. Meanwhile, the UCLA Grunwald Center for the Graphic Arts, also part of the Hammer, keeps more than 45,000 prints, drawings, photographs, and artists' books spanning the Renaissance to the present. Finally, to view the Hammer's fourth collection, stroll onto UCLA's North Campus to the Franklin D. Murphy Sculpture Garden. More than 70 sculptures, both figural and abstract, are installed across some five acres, including works by Jean Arp, David Smith, Auguste Rodin, Alexander Calder, and Barbara Hepworth.

Highlights:

Salomé Dancing Before Herod (1876), by French symbolist Gustave Moreau

Rembrandt van Rijn's *Juno* (1662–1665)

The famous woodcut by Katsushika Hokusai, *Fuji Behind the Waves off Kanagawa (The Great Wave)* (1831–1833)

Melencolia I (1514), the engraving by Albrecht Dürer

The full-length portrait *Dr. Pozzo at Home* (1881), by John Singer Sargent

UCLA Fowler Museum of Cultural History

405 Hilgard Avenue, North Campus, University of California,
Los Angeles (Map No. 1)
310-825-4361
www.fowler.ucla.edu

Open: W and F–Su, Noon–5:00 PM; Th, Noon–8:00 PM
Admission: Free
Parking: Pay parking in campus lots

One of America's premiere collections of non-Western art and
material culture can be found at this on-campus museum of the
University of California, Los Angeles. Founded in 1963 as the
Museum Laboratories of Ethnic Arts and Technology, the
museum seeks to explore the diverse cultures, both past and
present, of Native and Latin America, Asia and the Pacific,
and Africa and the African diaspora. It currently holds more
than 750,000 ethnographic and archaeological objects—from
elaborate Yoruban beadwork to Javanese puppetry, pre-
Columbian ceramics to post-apartheid South African election
materials. Also gathered here are more than 10,000 works of
cloth from across five continents and spanning two millennia,
making the museum a major repository for the textile arts.
Items are rotated into temporary shows as well as the museum's
newly organized, long-term exhibition, *Intersections: World Arts,
Local Lives*, which features highlights of the permanent collection to examine how art functions as a means for communication, empowerment, and transformation in cultures around the
world. At the museum, visitors can also view, on permanent
display, the silver collection of inventor Francis E. Fowler, Jr.,

whose family's major support to the museum is given recognition in the museum's name. This collection includes some 250 works of silver from 16th- through 19th-century Europe and the United States, including vessels from the workshops of Karl Fabergé and Paul Revere.

Highlights:

A rare 19th-century mask from the Bamileke peoples of Cameroon

"Nkisi Nkondi" power figure from the Yombe peoples of the Democratic Republic of the Congo (c. 18th to 19th century)

Ancient Moche portrait vessel from Peru (c. 100–800 CE)

An elaborate hornbill figure from Iban, Borneo (19th century)

University Art Museum, CSU Long Beach

1250 Bellflower Boulevard, Long Beach (Map No. 3)
562-985-5761
www.csulb.edu/uam

Open: During academic year—Tu–F, Noon–5:00 PM; Th, Noon–8:00 PM; Sa–Su, 11:00 AM–4:00 PM; during summer months—Tu–Sa, Noon–5:00 PM
Admission: General, $4.00
Parking: Pay parking in campus lots

Residing on the campus of the California State University, Long Beach, this museum presents changing exhibitions of contemporary art throughout the year, many featuring the work of underrepresented artists and all of them mounted to promote cross-cultural understanding through art. One recent exhibition, *phil collins: assume freedom*, featured new photography and video by British artist Phil Collins taken in areas of the world plagued by conflict. Selected works from the museum's permanent collection are on view on occasion, usually between temporary exhibitions. Its Gordon F. Hampton Collection consists of 85 works by 42 artists, including Al Held, Michael Goldberg, Adolph Gottlieb, Lee Krasner, and Milton Resnick. Works on paper in the museum's collection include photographs and prints by April Gornik, John Baldessari, Robert Rauschenberg, David Hockney, Lorna Simpson, Julius Shulman, and Candida Höfer. Finally, more than 20 site-specific sculptures, also belonging to the collection, are installed across the university's 322-acre campus.

USC Fisher Gallery

823 Exposition Boulevard, University of Southern California,
Los Angeles (Map No. 1)
213-740-4561
www.usc.edu/fishergallery

Open: During academic year (approximately September–mid-May),
Tu–Sa, Noon–5:00 PM; during summer by appointment only
Admission: Free
Parking: Pay parking in nearby lots; also street parking

This museum—founded in 1939 by Elizabeth Holmes Fisher, the University of Southern California's first woman trustee—has the distinction of being the first museum in Los Angeles to focus exclusively on fine art. In its collection are American Hudson River landscapes; 16th- and 17th-century Dutch, Flemish, and Italian masterworks; 18th-century British portraiture; French Barbizon paintings from the 1800s; and works on paper, sculptures, and paintings from the last century. The museum also has a growing collection of 20th- and 21st-century works by artists from California, Mexico, and Spain, including paintings, prints, drawings, and photographs. Selected works are displayed in changing exhibitions throughout the year, which range in subject from Old Master masterpieces to latest works by living artists, both local and international. A reading room makes pertinent literature available to visitors wishing to learn more about the art on view. During the school year, the museum also shows work by USC's fine-arts students.

Highlight:

Jenny Holzer's sculpture garden, *Blacklist*, a monument to the First Amendment and a memorial to the Hollywood Ten

The Wally Parks NHRA Motorsports Museum

1101 W. McKinley Avenue, Building 3A, Pomona (Map No. 4)

909-622-2133

www.nhra.com/museum

Open: W–Su, 10:00 AM–5:00 PM

Admission: Adults, $5.00; Seniors and Children 6–15, $3.00; Current NHRA Members and Children 5 and under, Free

Parking: Free in museum lot

Wally Parks was the longtime editor of *Hot Rod* magazine and the founder, in 1951, of the National Hot Rod Association (NHRA). This influential organization helped legitimize drag racing—long looked down upon as an illegal, unsafe street activity—and is today the largest sanctioning body in all of motorsports. In April of 1998, Parks opened the doors of a museum that salutes automotive speed and style in all of its forms. At any given time, one can check out some 80 vintage and modern cars on display, along with racing-related photographs, trophies, helmets, driving uniforms, and works of art by premiere motorsports illustrators. Come on the first Wednesday of the month from April to September for the museum's Twilight Cruise Nights, where street and professional racers as well as car enthusiasts gather to ooh and aah over the hottest hot rods in California.

Warner Bros. Museum

3400 Riverside Drive, Burbank (Map No. 2)
818-972-8687
www.wbstudio.com

Open: Access to museum by guided VIP studio tour only, offered every half hour—October–April, M–F, 9:00 AM–3:00 PM (last departure); May–September, M–F, 9:00 AM–4:00 PM (last departure)
Admission: General, $39.00; no one under 8 admitted
Parking: Pay parking in VIP Tour Center lot

From the very first talkies to silver-screen gems like *Casablanca*, television's beloved *The Dukes of Hazzard* to hit shows on the air today, the productions of Warner Bros. Studios span more than 80 years of entertainment. This museum displays memorabilia illustrating the studio's colorful history, especially its most famous properties. Countless scripts, costumes, casting reports, film clips, awards, correspondence, and other archival materials are rotated into changing exhibitions throughout the year. Recently, the museum celebrated the 50th anniversary of television by showcasing a half-century of Warner Bros. on the tube. Upstairs, J.K. Rowling fans of all ages will enjoy a long-term exhibition about Harry Potter, featuring wardrobe and props (including the magical "sorting hat" from the Hogwarts School of Witchcraft and Wizardry) used in the blockbuster film adaptations. Located right on the busy Warner Bros. lot, the museum is only accessible as part of the studio's 75-minute guided VIP tour.

Wells Fargo History Museum

333 S. Grand Avenue, Los Angeles (Map No. 1)
213-253-7166
www.wellsfargohistory.com/museums

Open: M–F, 9:00 AM–5:00 PM
Admission: Free
Parking: Pay parking in facility garage; also street parking

"Ocean to Ocean and Over the Seas" was the longtime slogan of the company Henry Wells and William Fargo founded in 1852. Sure enough, it went far and wide, bringing banking, communication, and transportation services to even the most remote cities, farms, and mining camps of the West. Whether by stagecoach, steamship, railroad, pony rider, or telegraph, customers relied on Wells Fargo to exchange gold, mail a package, or catch a ride along one of its extensive transcontinental stage routes, which at one point stretched over 3,000 miles. At this museum, located on the ground floor of downtown's skyscraping Wells Fargo Tower, the rise of the company is explored in the context of this early regional history. Vintage photographs, maps, bills of exchange, gold coins, mining tools, balance scales, telegraphs, buckskin bags, passenger documents, Western fine art, among hundreds of other artifacts, illustrate the life and times of those who pioneered the West and the ways the Wells Fargo companies sought to serve their needs.

Highlights:

An authentic Concord Coach (active 1898–1917)

The 100-ounce gold Challenge Nugget

The Wende Museum

5741 Buckingham Parkway, Suite E, Culver City (Map No. 1)
310-216-1600
www.wendemuseum.org

Open: First and third Friday of the month, 9:00 AM–5:00 PM
Admission: Free
Parking: Free in museum lot; also street parking

Driving through a run-of-the-mill Culver City office park, you wouldn't expect to stumble upon a bright, artfully painted portion of the Berlin Wall. Yet the tall relic flanks the entrance of this museum, which, since its opening in 2002, has served as a repository for objects and archives relating to Eastern Europe and the Soviet Union during the Cold War (1945–1991). For more than a decade, the museum's founder and director, Justinian Jampol, has spearheaded a diligent, passionate effort to identify, document, and — when possible and appropriate — acquire artifacts and artworks reflecting the extinct cultures of the former Eastern Bloc, many of which had faced the threat of deterioration, vandalism, or dismantlement. The museum's collection includes Social Realist oil paintings; statuettes and busts of Vladimir Lenin and other communist leaders; more than 500 ceremonial plates bearing the seals of various government, quasi-official, and civilian organizations of Eastern Europe; secret police files; and pennants, toys, medals, and assorted memorabilia of the Freie Deutsche Jugend (Free German Youth). Throughout the museum, attention is paid to the particular visual language used to maintain and advance socialist ideology. A tour of the museum's vault, held daily at 3:00 PM, shows visitors even more of what Jampol and his team have collected over the years.

Additional highlights:

A handcarved sculpture (1954) portraying the "proletarian elite" — the farmer, the engineer, and the tradesman — that used to be in the State Council Building of East Berlin

The street signs for Zimmerstrasse and Friedrichstrasse, the intersection where the Checkpoint Charlie border crossing was situated

So-called "initative posters" and other works of graphic arts encouraging citizens to work hard, produce more, and beware of foreign influences

Western Museum of Flight

12016 Prairie Avenue, Jack Northrop Field, Hawthorne Municipal
Airport, Hawthorne (Map No. 1)
310-332-6228
www.wmof.com

Open: Tu–Sa, 10:00 AM–3:00 PM
Admission: Adults, $5.00; Children under 12, Free
Parking: Free in facility lot

The buzz of small aircraft taking off and landing within earshot
is a reminder of the industry this museum seeks to honor.
Located on the grounds of a municipal airport, it welcomes
visitors of all ages to enjoy the heritage of military aircraft, with
emphasis on Southern California's impact on aviation history.
The museum displays vintage aircraft, engines, World War II
instruments, aircrew accessories, memorabilia, documents, and
photographs. Here one can view a 1942 mode C-3 Link
Trainer, an early World War II–era flight simulator that helped
train more than half a million airmen during and after the war.
Outside, children and grown-ups alike can experience aircraft
up close. Stand beside a YF-17 fighting plane, the prototype for
the present-day FA-18 Hornet, or climb the steep aisle to the
cockpit of a restored DC-3, one of the first successful commercial aircrafts. The Darrell G. McNeal Restoration Facility,
dedicated to restoring and preserving aircraft, is also a part of
the museum.

Highlights:

A chance to sit behind the controls of an F-14 "Tomcat" fighter plane

A still-operational World War II P-51 "Mustang"

Whittier Museum

6755 Newlin Avenue, Whittier (Map No. 4)
562-945-3871
www.whittiermuseum.org

Open: Access to museum by guided tour only, offered Sa–Su,
1:00–4:00 PM, or during the week by appointment
Recommended donation: General, $3.00–$5.00
Parking: Free in museum lot

In 1886, Chicago businessman Aquilla Pickering traveled to
California in search of a location for a West Coast Quaker
colony. Along with several fellow Society of Friends members,
he acquired ranch land that would later be incorporated as the
city of Whittier. Located in historic "uptown," this museum
recalls early life in Whittier, starting from its Quaker origins.
On the ground floor, photographs, historical artifacts, memorabilia, farm tools, and assorted personal items are organized
into themed rooms—a replica of a Quaker meeting house, for
example, contains an exhibit about sacred spaces in the city
over the years, while a re-created barn focuses on the town's
early reliance on agriculture and oil. Upstairs, in addition to a
tribute to the American soldier from the Revolutionary War
to the present, are galleries dedicated to two prominent
Whittier figures—Pio Pico, the last Mexican governor of
California, and President Richard M. Nixon.

Highlights:

A shaving box of Abraham Lincoln's given to a friend in
Illinois, passed down through generations

The door to the museum's archives, taken from the entrance of
Whittier's original public library

William S. Hart Museum

24151 San Fernando Road, Newhall (Map No. 2)

661-254-4584

www.hartmuseum.org

Open: Labor Day through mid-June, W–F, 10:00 AM–1:00 PM and
Sa–Su, 11:00 AM–4:00 PM; mid-June through Labor Day, W–Su,
11:00 AM–4:00 PM; park only, 7:00 AM–sunset

Admission: Free

Parking: Free in facility lot

A silent Western made between 1914 and 1925 may very well
have starred William Surrey Hart (1864–1946) as the bad guy.
In 1925, upon retiring from making films, Hart built a hilltop
home in Newhall and called it La Loma de Los Vientos, or
"the hill of the winds." The house was completed in 1927 and
Hart lived there until his death. By last will and testament, he
left the house and the 265-acre property on which it stands to
Los Angeles County, specifying that they be dedicated as a
museum and a park for the public to enjoy at no charge. The
Spanish Colonial Revival mansion contains all of the original
furnishings and Hart's personal effects, providing insight into
his life. Hart's great love of animals is evidenced, for example,
by the sizeable bedroom of his two Harlequin Great Danes
and the prominently displayed portrait, painted by James
Montgomery Flagg, of Hart and his beloved pinto pony and
frequent co-star, Fritz. Hart was an avid collector of Western
American art, so throughout the house are bronze sculptures,
illustrations, and paintings by Charles Russell, Frederic
Remington, Charles Christadoro, Joe De Young, and other
premiere artists of the genre. Hart's collection of Native

American artifacts and textiles is also on view, as are costumes, props, photographs, and other memorabilia from his Hollywood days.

The nature trail up to La Loma de Los Vientos takes about 15 minutes so wear comfortable shoes. Along the way, you may catch a glimpse of the American bison that roam the ranch, descendants of a herd donated to the park by Walt Disney in 1962. At the foot of the hill is the Ranch House, which contains original furnishings, memorabilia, and riding equipment used in some of Hart's movies.

Highlights:

A bearskin rug shot by Mrs. Will Rogers

An American flag that Amelia Earhart had in her possession on her 1928 transatlantic flight and which she signed and gave to Hart, her dear friend

Workman and Temple Family Homestead Museum

15415 E. Don Julian Road, City of Industry (Map No. 4)
626-968-8492
www.homesteadmuseum.org

Open: Access to houses by guided tour only, offered hourly, W–Su,
1:00–4:00 PM
Admission: Free
Parking: Free in museum lot

In 1841, Englishman William Workman and his family settled
in the rural area that would become City of Industry. With the
success of their cattle ranch, vineyards, and wheat farm, the
Workmans were able to invest in remodeling the modest house
they had built upon arriving in Southern California. What
started out as a three-room adobe expanded, over the next 30
years, into a modern, two-story American country home, likely
the work of early Los Angeles architect Ezra Kysor. Today the
Workman House is a California State Historic Landmark, significant for reflecting domestic architectural tastes of mid-19th-
century America. Just next door is La Casa Nueva, the 1920s
Spanish Colonial Revival mansion of William Workman's
grandson Walter Temple. A commissioned work by the architectural firm of Walker & Eisen and later Roy Seldon Price,
the 11,000-square-foot residence has nearly 50 stained-glass
windows, many of which illustrate the history of the Temple
family. Taken together, these works represent the largest public
collection of its kind in California. The last site to visit at the
museum is El Campo Santo, one of the oldest cemeteries in
Southern California, where Workman and Temple family

members have been laid to rest and to which the remains of Pio Pico, the last Mexican governor of California, were relocated in the 1920s.

Highlight:

The stained-glass tryptich above the entry hall staircase, romantically depicting crowds of missionaries and settlers along the California coast eagerly awaiting the arrival of Spanish galleons

Zimmer Children's Museum

6505 Wilshire Boulevard, Suite 100, Los Angeles (Map No. 1)

323-761-8989

www.zimmermuseum.org

Open: T, 10:00 AM–5:00 PM; W–Th and Su, 12:30–5:00 PM; F, 10:00
AM–12:30 PM
Admission: Adults, $5.00; Children 3–12, $3.00; Children under 3,
Free; Grandparents, Free when accompanied by a grandchild
Parking: Free limited parking in adjacent lot

Playing while learning about community is what this children's
museum hopes every visitor experiences. Taking inspiration
from traditional Jewish values, such as *tikkun olam* (repairing the
world) and *tzedakah* (justice), the exhibits encourage families of
all backgrounds to consider how we can make a difference in
the world. The Mann Theater, for example, not only gives
young ones a chance to dress up and perform in virtual settings
thanks to blue-screen technology, but also offers a way to
examine how our roles and behaviors affect those around us. In
other exhibits, kids can board the "Zimmer Plane" and imagine the joy of meeting people from all over the world, or pre-
tend to answer a call for help in "The Ambulance" and show
compassion for those in need. There are also educational games
promoting everything from water conservation to music appreciation.

Additional highlight:
A replica of Jerusalem's Western Wall where children can leave
their hopes and wishes for the future

Appendix

The following lists are thematic guides to the museums located in Los Angeles. All lists are in alphabetical order.

The Hollywood Museum

L. Ron Hubbard Life Exhibition

The Museum of Jurassic Technology

Museum of Neon Art

Page Museum at the La Brea Tar Pits

Schindler House (see entry for the MAK Center for Art and Architecture)

Warner Bros. Museum

The Wende Museum

Ten Museums for Children

California Science Center

Children's Museum of Los Angeles

Kidspace Children's Museum

Los Angeles Live Steamers Railroad Museum

Natural History Museum of Los Angeles County

Skirball Cultural Center's new family gallery

Page Museum at La Brea Tar Pits

Raymond M. Alf Museum of Paleontology

Travel Town Transportation Museum

Zimmer Children's Museum

Ten Museums — Art and Architecture

The Huntington Library, Art Collections, and Botanical Gardens

J. Paul Getty Museum (see entries for the Getty Center and the Getty Villa)

Long Beach Museum of Art

Los Angeles County Museum of Art

The Museum of Contemporary Art

Museum of Latin American Art

Norton Simon Museum

Pacific Asia Museum

UCLA Armand Hammer Museum and Cultural Center

USC Fisher Gallery

Ten Museums — American History

Autry National Center: Museum of the American West

Autry National Center: Southwest Museum of the American Indian

California African American Museum

Chinese American Museum

Civil Rights Museum

Drum Barracks Civil War Museum

Japanese American National Museum

Fort MacArthur Museum

Petersen Automotive Museum

The S.S. *Lane Victory* Museum

Ten Museums — Regional Interest

Autry National Center: Museum of the American West

California Heritage Museum

Drum Barracks Civil War Museum

Fort MacArthur Museum

Los Angeles Fire Department Museum

Los Angeles Maritime Museum

Los Angeles Police Museum

Pasadena Museum of California Art

San Gabriel Mission Museum

Wells Fargo History Museum

Ten Museums — Science and Technology

California Science Center

International Printing Museum

Museum of Flying

Museum of Television and Radio

Natural History Museum of Los Angeles County

Page Museum at the La Brea Tar Pits

Petersen Automotive Museum

The Paul Gray PC Museum

Raymond M. Alf Museum of Paleontology

Western Museum of Flight

Ten Museums—Historic Houses

Adamson House and Malibu Lagoon Museum

Andres Pico Adobe

Avila Adobe

Banning Residence Museum

The Gamble House

Heritage Square Museum

Hollyhock House

Muller House Museum

Pasadena Museum of History

Schindler House (see entry for the MAK Center for Art and Architecture)

Ten Museums—Ethnic or Cultural Interest

Ararat-Eskijian Museum

Antelope Valley Indian Museum

Autry National Center: Southwest Museum of the American Indian

California African American Museum

Chinese American Museum

Japanese American National Museum

Korean Cultural Center

La Historia Society/Museo de los Barrios

Skirball Cultural Center

UCLA Fowler Museum of Cultural History

Museums that Require Appointments

The Bunny Museum

The Cake Lady's ® Mini Cake Museum

Canoga-Owensmouth Historical Museum

Civil Rights Museum

The Getty Villa

Kenneth G. Fiske Museum of the Claremont Colleges

Warner Bros. Museum

Index of Alternative Museum Names